What People Are Saying About Apostle Guillermo Maldonado and *Jesus Is Coming Soon...*

My friend Apostle Guillermo Maldonado is one of the most important voices in America and beyond. His passion for Jesus is contagious. He speaks with great authority and wisdom as he lives acutely aware of the times in which we are living as the church in this world. I highly recommend this faithful servant of the Lord and the message he carries for us all.

—*Bill Johnson*
Bethel Church, Redding, CA
Author of numerous books, including *When Heaven Invades Earth* and *The Way of Life*

In *Jesus Is Coming Soon*, Apostle Guillermo Maldonado stresses, "This generation is on the verge of seeing the greatest outpouring of the Holy Spirit and the greatest revival in history. The remnant church is about to enter into the glory of God.... The earth began with the glory of God manifested in creation, and it will end with the glory manifested in the supernatural wonders of the last days, which God is about to reveal." This book shows how you can participate in God's greatest revival and see the manifestations of His glory during these momentous last days before the return of Jesus Christ!

—*Paula White-Cain*
Paula White Ministries
Evangelist and Senior Pastor
New Destiny Christian Center, Orlando, FL

My friend Apostle Guillermo Maldonado brilliantly prepares you to be part of God's end-time remnant. It is one minute to midnight. Time is running out!

—*Sid Roth*
Host, *It's Supernatural!*

The end of the age is no longer approaching—it is upon us. How should we conduct ourselves in these last days to fulfill God's eternal purpose and provide an example to a world that is looking for answers? In *Jesus Is Coming Soon*, Apostle Guillermo Maldonado offers hope and inspiration with apostolic authority, prophetic clarity, and unmistakable urgency.

—*Dr. Rod Parsley*
Pastor and Founder
World Harvest Church, Columbus, OH

Are you ready? Are you prepared for what is coming in the last days and at the end of the age? The phrase *Maranatha* was on the lips of the early disciples as they lived this life in preparation for the next. These electric words should not only be on our lips, too, but they should be a living reality in our hearts and lifestyles. In *Jesus Is Coming Soon*, Apostle Guillermo Maldonado clearly shows us how to live in light of eternity during these end times. Each of us must make sure we are ready for the final act of the greatest story ever told—the second coming of the Lord Jesus Christ. The Spirit and the bride say, "Come!" Even so, come, our dear Lord Jesus Christ!

—*Dr. James W. Goll*
Founder, God Encounters Ministries
GOLL Ideation LLC

Jesus Is Coming Soon is an important book. Many people are confused about basic biblical truth. The reality is that Jesus is coming soon, just as Apostle Maldonado clearly states. Because of this fact, reaching the world for Christ is one of our central mandates. One simply cannot read this book without finding one's heart burning for lost souls as well as longing for our Savior's return.

—*Cindy Jacobs*
Generals International

I love Guillermo Maldonado and his passion to bring back the urgency of Christ's return as a central focus of the church. So many Christians are consumed with living out a destiny now without any regard to living for our eternal destiny: being with Jesus where He is. As he shares his perspective, Guillermo always points to eternity, and this causes people to have greater hope than if they were just hearing about how to live out their salvation in this turbulent world. We need the higher focus of our everlasting life motivating us in the now. We also need Jesus to be the center of this eternal focus, and *Jesus Is Coming Soon* helps to reframe our view while also guiding us like a compass. There are so many different perspectives about how Jesus will return and what that day will look like. Even if your theological perspective differs, I encourage you to read this book to gain new passion and live with eternity in view in your everyday life.

—*Shawn Bolz*
Host, *Translating God* television program
Host, *Exploring the Prophetic* podcast
Author, *Translating God, God Secrets*, and *Through the Eyes of Love*
www.bolzministries.com

It is truly an honor to endorse Apostle Guillermo Maldonado's new book, *Jesus Is Coming Soon*. Within these pages, you will discover specific keys to unlock your understanding of the current times and seasons. You will also gain remarkable prophetic insights into the end-time signs that are all around us. This book will aid you in attaining stability during the unprecedented shakings we are seeing. I have had the honor to travel the earth for over fifty-five years, speaking an average of five times a week. During these years, I have met many godly people. Apostle Maldonado is one of these very special people. I have the highest respect and admiration for him. His character and integrity are top-notch. I wholeheartedly recommend this timely and inspired book.

—*Prophet Bobby Conner*
Eagles View Ministries
www.bobbyconner.org

Apostle Guillermo Maldonado has written many books concerning the foundations of biblical truth, victorious Christian living, how to manifest the supernatural, and how to be established in the present purposes of God on earth. It is absolutely essential that every Christian read his new book, *Jesus Is Coming Soon*. All scriptural end-time signs regarding the world, Israel, and the church are coming to a climax. By reading this book, you will discover how to be properly prepared to co-labor with Christ in completing the final things that must be fulfilled for Jesus to return (Acts 3:21). Bless you, Guillermo, for providing such a valuable book for the Holy Spirit to use to prepare the church for Christ's return.

—*Bishop Bill Hamon*
Christian International Apostolic-Global Network
Author of numerous books, including *The Eternal Church*, *Prophets and Personal Prophecy*, and *Prophets and the Prophetic Movement*

JESUS IS COMING SOON

DISCERN THE END-TIME SIGNS AND PREPARE FOR HIS RETURN

GUILLERMO MALDONADO

JESUS IS COMING SOON

DISCERN THE END-TIME SIGNS AND PREPARE FOR HIS RETURN

WHITAKER HOUSE

Unless otherwise indicated, all Scripture quotations are taken from the *New King James Version*, © 1979, 1980, 1982, 1984 by Thomas Nelson, Inc. Used by permission. Scripture quotation marked (KJV) is taken from the King James Version of the Holy Bible. Scripture quotation marked (AMP) is taken from *The Amplified® Bible*, © 2015 by The Lockman Foundation, La Habra, CA. Used by permission. (www.Lockman.org). All rights reserved.

Boldface type in the Scripture quotations indicates the author's emphasis.

The forms LORD and GOD (in small caps) in Bible quotations represent the Hebrew name for God *Yahweh* (JEHOVAH), while LORD and GOD normally represent the name *Adonai*, in accordance with the Bible version used.

Unless otherwise noted, definitions of Hebrew and Greek words are taken from the electronic version of *Strong's Exhaustive Concordance of the Bible*, STRONG (© 1980, 1986, and assigned to World Bible Publishers, Inc. Used by permission. All rights reserved.). The definition of the Greek word for *"nation," ethnos,* in chapter 5 is taken from the New Testament Greek Lexicon—King James Version, based on Thayer's and Smith's Bible Dictionary, plus others (public domain), https://www.biblestudytools.com/lexicons/greek/kjv/ethnos.html.

Unless otherwise indicated, all dictionary definitions are taken from *Merriam-Webster.com*, 2020.

All Voice of the Martyrs article summaries and quotations in this book are used by permission of Voice of the Martyrs Australia. Barna Group statistics and quotes used by permission. Pew Research Center bears no responsibility for the analyses or interpretations of its data presented in this book. The opinions expressed herein, including any implications for policy, are those of the author and not of Pew Research Center.

ERJ Credits:
Editors: Jose M. Anhuaman and Vanesa Vargas
Editorial development: Gloria Zura
Cover design: Caroline Pereira

JESUS IS COMING SOON:
DISCERN THE END-TIME SIGNS AND PREPARE FOR HIS RETURN

Guillermo Maldonado
13651 S.W. 143rd Ct., #101 • Miami, FL 33186
http://kingjesusministry.org/
www.ERJPub.org

ISBN: 978-1-64123-501-3 • eBook ISBN: 978-1-64123-502-0
Printed in the United States of America
© 2020 by Guillermo Maldonado

Whitaker House • 1030 Hunt Valley Circle • New Kensington, PA 15068
www.whitakerhouse.com

Library of Congress Control Number: 2020942361

1 2 3 4 5 6 7 8 9 10 11 **ᏣᎻ** 27 26 25 24 23 22 21 20

CONTENTS

FOREWORD

We are living in unusual times. Communities and nations are facing distressing circumstances that baffle the minds of men. Paul wrote to Timothy, *"This know also, that in the last days perilous times shall come"* (2 Timothy 3:1 KJV). Many perplexing events are unfolding at a rapid rate, and the world has no answers to these dilemmas. Scientists and politicians don't have the solutions because such issues have a spiritual root that only God can address.

As you and I live in the midst of these exceptional times, the question isn't so much, "What is happening?" but rather, "Why are these things happening?" They are occurring because Jesus is returning soon, and this world is coming to its culmination. The extraordinary events we are seeing are not taking place by accident. God is carrying out His purposes and plans, which are progressing according to His own design. And every end-time sign indicates that Jesus's coming is drawing nearer and nearer.

Unfortunately, many people in the church today have not acknowledged this fact. They have mainly adopted a political mindset, relying on human solutions to the world's problems. As a result, they are losing their spirituality. They are no longer focused on Jesus Christ and the power of God to save, heal, and deliver. As believers, we are meant to *"walk circumspectly, not as fools, but as wise, redeeming the time, because the days are evil. Wherefore be ye not unwise, but understanding what the will of the Lord is"* (Ephesians 5:15–17 KJV).

Apostle Guillermo Maldonado is one of the apostles of the new millennium. He has always been on the cutting edge of what is happening today. I am so grateful that the Lord has put it upon him to write this book on the end times. *Jesus Is Coming Soon* will open this generation's eyes to the revelation of the coming of Christ and to the signs of our time.

Years ago, many people used to consider "the end times" as just another doctrine of the church to believe. However, today, we have no choice but to recognize that Jesus's second coming is not mere doctrine. It is a reality. Everything that is occurring on earth in preparation for Christ's return is happening the way Jesus said it would happen. The events of the last days are exposing the evil work of Satan, the perilous state of mankind, and the identity of God's remnant.

I believe that as you read *Jesus Is Coming Soon*, you will be enlightened to these truths, and you will recognize the part God has given you to play in the end times.

Open your heart and expect to be confronted and changed.

—*Apostle Renny McLean*
Renny McLean Ministries

PREFACE: A CALL TO BE PART OF GOD'S REMNANT

For a long while, I have sensed in my spirit that the time of Jesus's coming is drawing near. As I explain throughout this book, both the prophetic Scriptures and the movement of the Holy Spirit in our midst today reveal that Christ is almost at the door. I am passionate about serving the Lord with all my heart and ministering His supernatural power and glory in the world during the time that is remaining.

I have felt an urgency to write this book so that all people can discern the end-time signs of Christ's appearing and prepare for it. Although the signs of the end of the age and Jesus's return are evident in the physical and spiritual worlds, most people, including Christians, have not recognized them. This book will unfold:

+ The reason for the unprecedented natural and spiritual shakings in our world

- What the signs (including unusual occurrences such as blood moons) tell us

- How God works according to seasons, eras, and the fullness of time

- How Jewish feasts point to the ages of man, accurately showing us God's timetable

- Which imminent biblical signs and promises have yet to be fulfilled

- The judgments God is bringing to the earth

Biblical end-times prophecies speak of faithful followers of Jesus who are called the "remnant." These are the believers who are ready for the last days and Jesus's return. However, the Scriptures also speak of people who are unprepared for His appearing or fall away from their faith beforehand.

Let me ask you this crucial question: which prophecy will you fulfill? Are you part of the end-time remnant?

Jesus Is Coming Soon will help you be certain you are part of God's remnant. I pray that all Christians will return to their *"first love"* (Revelation 2:4) and recommit themselves to their heavenly Father during this time. The Holy Spirit is disclosing God's last-days purposes right now. We must know how to receive the vital revelation and prophetic knowledge He wants to share with His people. When we have this foreknowledge, we can understand the times and prepare for God's final plans for the earth.

Through this book, I want to seriously challenge you to examine your life and faith. I believe your spiritual future is at stake. But I also want to assure you that, in these end times, you do not need to be fearful, discouraged, or distracted. Instead, you can know your true position in God before Christ appears. You can be joyfully prepared, watching and waiting in expectation, with your spiritual eyes open.

God intends the church to be a community of hope, revival, and supernatural power in the midst of the dark times in our world. People must turn to God for the answers only He can give, and the church needs to be ready to provide those answers. I urge you to live in God's perfect will for your life, discern the times, and participate in His supernatural, last-days purposes!

"Surely I am coming quickly." Amen. Even so, come, Lord Jesus!

(Revelation 22:20)

CHAPTER 1

KNOWING THE TIMES AND SEASONS

God often prompts a necessary change in our lives by leading us to ask essential questions. In recent times, we have been experiencing unsettling events—the rapid emergence of the coronavirus, with all its medical, economic, and governmental repercussions; disturbances in our physical environment, such as intense hurricanes and melting glaciers; political uncertainty and unrest; and much more. We need to be asking ourselves questions like these:

+ What is happening in our world?

+ Is there a relationship between the spiritual world and the natural phenomena we see occurring?

+ Where are we today on God's prophetic timetable for the end times and the return of Jesus Christ?

- What do we need to know about God's agendas for the church, the nation of Israel, and the world at large during the last days?

- Which spiritual season is the church going through right now— and which season is about to come? Is the church ready for these seasons?

- If Jesus's second coming is near, what should believers be doing right now to prepare for this momentous event?

I ask you to seriously consider these questions and join me in discovering the answers to them. God is moving in unprecedented ways today. This is not a time when we can sit on the sidelines and simply watch. The body of Christ—and each individual believer—has a tremendous role and responsibility in what is happening and about to happen in our world. But in order to carry out this role, we must first address a deep and disturbing problem in the church.

A LACK OF REVEALED KNOWLEDGE AND PROPHECY

The modern church has many deficiencies, but above all, it has a great lack of revealed knowledge and understanding of prophecy. In these times, it is dangerous to live in such ignorance. God said something thousands of years ago through the prophet Hosea that is relevant to us today: *"My people are destroyed for lack of knowledge"* (Hosea 4:6).

It's alarming how unfamiliar the church is with God's end-time purposes because of this absence of revelation and prophecy. People are walking blindly when they greatly need spiritual sight. Most believers are not prepared for what is coming. They don't recognize the spiritual season in which God is working. They are like the foolish virgins in Jesus's parable who fell asleep while waiting for the bridegroom and forgot to make sure they had enough oil in their lamps. Consequently, they were shut out of the wedding feast. (See Matthew 25:1–13.) We must wake up, make sure our "lamps" are filled, and be ready for our Bridegroom when He comes!

THE NECESSITY OF SPIRITUAL REVELATION

The times and seasons of our physical earth are governed by natural laws. We are very familiar with them because they are part of the world around us. We recognize them by our physical senses or know about them through discoveries in the field of science, which has advanced far. However, there are supernatural seasons of a divine nature that we can only recognize through spiritual revelation. Many events and happenings today are linked to the spiritual realm. Thus, we cannot comprehend them without discernment from the Holy Spirit. These are days in which we need revealed knowledge more than common sense, which is limited by what we can see and hear in the physical realm. Without revealed knowledge, we cannot function in God's "now"—that is, everything He is doing and planning *today*. Through revelation, we discover God's now.

We often hear the phrase "history repeats itself." However, in our times, there don't seem to be any historical references to help explain some of the events that are occurring. We have entered a period of unusual and sudden manifestations for which we have no previous orientation. Therefore, natural man cannot predict these events or foresee how they will unfold. We might be able to describe them when they occur, but their meaning remains unclear to us. Only those who have the revelation of the Holy Spirit will be able to understand their implications. *"For this reason I will not be negligent to remind you always of these things, though you know and are established in the present truth"* (2 Peter 1:12).

THREE LEVELS OF SPIRITUAL KNOWLEDGE

The Bible provides us with three levels of knowledge: *fundamental*, *revelational*, and *prophetic*. Even though they serve different purposes, they are each an essential part of the prophetic communications God gives for His people and the world.

FUNDAMENTAL KNOWLEDGE

God gives us fundamental spiritual knowledge through the teachings and examples of the written Scriptures, the Bible. The Bible is the record of God's covenantal relationship with His people throughout history, the unfolding of His plans to redeem the world through Jesus Christ, the Messiah, and His clear instructions for how we are to live our lives in love, honor, and obedience toward Him. The Bible also contains prophecy, which I discuss under "Prophetic Knowledge" below. Through the Scriptures, the Holy Spirit continually speaks to us about the essentials of God's nature, will, and ways.

REVELATIONAL KNOWLEDGE

Revelational knowledge discloses even more of God's mysteries. God's Spirit removes the veil from spiritual realities so we can see His current divine purposes and activities, which are hidden to the natural or fallen human mind. The apostle Paul never ceased to pray that the believers in the churches he had established would live according to revealed knowledge: *"that the God of our Lord Jesus Christ, the Father of glory, may give to you the spirit of wisdom and revelation in the knowledge of Him"* (Ephesians 1:17).

There are two important Greek words related to receiving revelation from God: *Logos* and *rhema*. Both terms refer to knowledge and wisdom from God, but they do so in different ways. The *Logos* is the written Word of God, which, from Genesis to Revelation, was inspired by the Holy Spirit. A *rhema* is a word from God for today, for a specific situation. A *rhema* word will always be in agreement with the *Logos* word. It will never contradict it. One example of a *rhema* word is when the Holy Spirit causes the written Scriptures to come alive in meaning for us, with application for our present circumstances. Another example is a prophetic word given through the Spirit for individual believers or the church.

What is the Spirit saying to us *now*? What do we need to know *now* to follow and serve God? The Holy Spirit continues to speak through the written Word, but He also brings additional revelation to the hearts of men and women of God who hear His voice. The Father sent the Spirit for this very purpose. (See John 14:26.) Most theologians do not understand this truth; they believe that everything God wants to say to us is recorded in the Bible.

Jesus fulfilled all the scriptural prophecies about the Messiah, and we have a written record in the New Testament of His life and teachings. However, the Bible tells us that He did many other things that were not written down. *"And there are also many other things that Jesus did, which if they were written one by one, I suppose that even the world itself could not contain the books that would be written"* (John 21:25). I believe that only the seeds of these other truths that Jesus spoke and demonstrated have remained, but now the Holy Spirit is revealing and opening them up for us, as well as other previously hidden truths. Again, the proof that these new revelations are genuine and come from God is that they never contradict the written Word.

Thus, revelation is the aspect of prophecy that is "now"; it is God telling us what He is doing today. Indeed, if it is not now, it is not revelation. Revelation is what keeps King Jesus Ministry relevant to the church and the world, always at the forefront of God's supernatural movement. In order for us to receive this revelation, it has been necessary to continually seek God and submit our wills to Him. As a result, spiritual realities have been opened that were not previously open to us. The same can occur in your life, church, and ministry.

THE PURPOSE OF REVEALED KNOWLEDGE IS TO OPEN OUR SPIRITUAL EYES AND UNDERSTANDING SO WE ARE AWARE OF THE TRUTHS AND INFORMATION GOD DESIRES TO GIVE US IN THE NOW.

PROPHETIC KNOWLEDGE

The third level, prophetic knowledge, refers to the prophecy contained in the Bible. Although there are different definitions of the word *prophecy*, I am using it in the sense of predictions about the future. The Scriptures tell us that *"the testimony of Jesus is the spirit of prophecy"* (Revelation 19:10). The "spirit of prophecy" from God is that which declares the future; it can be predictive about either a person, place, or thing. God is eternal, and He can reveal to us what will occur in the future. *"The four living creatures…do not rest day or night, saying: 'Holy, holy, holy, Lord God Almighty, who was and is and is to come!'"* (Revelation 4:8).

I want to reemphasize that understanding the prophecies in the Bible is one of the church's primary needs today, especially if we are to be relevant in our ministry to the world. If we do not know prophecy, we will not be able to comprehend what is occurring in the spiritual realm. Instead of having knowledge of biblical prophecy, the church has a lot of speculation and projection, which are merely products of human intelligence-gathering. Certain teachers and preachers want to predict the future using the precedents of the past. But again, that method will not work in God's now because what we are experiencing today is unparalleled in history.

"By faith Abraham obeyed when he was called to go out to the place which he would receive as an inheritance. And he went out, not knowing where he was going" (Hebrews 11:8). We cannot exercise faith for the future without having received some foresight or foreknowledge from God. Faith in Him for the events that are coming is born out of prophecy; it comes from knowing what will happen before it occurs. *"Now faith is the substance of things hoped for, the evidence of things not seen"* (verse 1).

THE PURPOSE OF PROPHECY IS TO REVEAL THE FUTURE SO WE CAN PREPARE FOR WHAT IS TO COME.

That means when we have this foreknowledge, we readily prepare, and we also obey what God has already revealed to us. For example, my job as an apostle is to prepare the bride, the church, for the second coming of the Son of God. I do this with the revelation and prophecy provided by the written Word and the voice of the Holy Spirit, who guides me and anticipates all that I need to fulfill this assignment.

Jesus is coming again, just as He promised! (See, for example, John 14:3.) If we are paying attention to God's Word, we know this is true because we believe the Scriptures and the revelation of the Holy Spirit. Therefore, we expect His return. But the world does not have this spiritual foreknowledge. That is why there is a great need for prophecy today to inform every area of society: church, family, government, business, education, science, and more.

Some preachers and Bible teachers deny or reject the person of the Holy Spirit and His work among God's people today. As a result, they have no avenue for understanding the signs of the times, either what is happening in the now or what will occur in the future. I will tell you this: it is not possible to know God's will for the now without the Holy Spirit. We can know the general will of the Lord through His written Word, but we cannot understand the prophetic Scriptures that correspond exactly to the now.

WHILE A *RHEMA* WORD IS A REVELATION FOR THE NOW, PROPHECY IS A WORD FOR THE FUTURE.

We must keep in mind that if we don't receive God's revelation and understand prophecy, we will struggle to live correctly and serve others in ministry during these crucial times. I believe that if we, as Christians, truly understood the season in which we are living, we would not become discouraged or distracted by activities that have no real spiritual value and that we were never called to do. Certain people believe that if prophecy is real, it applies to other people but not to them. It is not God's will for us to fumble around or apply His Word in any way we want, but rather for us to understand the prophecy He has given us, guided by His Word and Spirit.

THE MINISTRIES OF PROPHETS AND APOSTLES

Revelation and prophecy are two types of anointing from the Holy Spirit that will prepare the way for the second coming of Christ. The prophets of the Old Testament prepared the way for Jesus's first coming, and the apostles and prophets of the church today will help prepare the way for His second coming. They will reveal essential truths from God, just as the apostles and prophets in the first century helped the early church to understand the fullness of the gospel: *"Which in other ages was not made known to the sons of men, as it has now been revealed by the Spirit to His holy apostles and prophets"* (Ephesians 3:5).

Unfortunately, over the centuries, the ministries of the apostle and prophet were, in effect, lost from the everyday life of the church, and, with them, their unique gifts, which God provided to build up His people. God has given to apostles and prophets the ability to interpret the times and seasons in which we are living, and we need them as much as any other ministry of the church. Without them, we cannot apprehend God's mysteries and counsel, which would otherwise remain hidden.

In recent times, the Holy Spirit has been restoring these two ministries in the body of Christ. The apostles and prophets are coming together as a unified voice on earth, as a company that is preparing the way of the Lord. The prophets of old represent the first glory, and the apostles and prophets of today represent the final glory. The Holy Spirit is raising apostolic and prophetic voices to announce the appearing of Jesus Christ, bringing revelation to believers and preparing them to be the remnant that will usher in His coming.

WHAT MAKES A PROPHECY VALID?

A revelational prophecy isn't just any word that predicts the future. We must be careful because many voices are rising today to bring confusion and disbelief among believers and people in the world. For a prophecy to be valid, it must truly come from God. But how can we know that something we hear actually comes from Him? There are three indisputable bases for recognizing a true prophetic word: the Scriptures, the Holy Spirit, and the feasts of the Lord.

1. THE SCRIPTURES

We know that God's Word has yet to be fulfilled in its entirety, which gives the Scriptures their continuing prophetic nature. Whenever a prophecy in the Word is fulfilled, that aspect of the Bible becomes history. *"And so we have the prophetic word confirmed, which you do well to heed as a light that shines in a dark place, until the day dawns and the morning star rises in your hearts"* (2 Peter 1:19). Therefore, if all the prophecy in the Bible had already been fulfilled, we would be reading only a history book.

The prophetic aspect of the Scriptures is everything that has to do with God's promises and prophecies for the future. Everything the Bible announces that has not yet been fulfilled is something we should expect and look for. If we are not open to the prophetic, we are saying there is nothing of God's works left to see. We must not despise biblical prophecy or prophecies given by the Holy Spirit today. (See 1 Thessalonians 5:20.)

People in the church constantly seem to be divided over the God of history versus the God of the now, forgetting that He *"was and is and is to come!'"* (Revelation 4:8). If someone reads the Bible as a historical book alone, they will conclude that there will be no second coming of Jesus Christ. There are many preachers who do not believe in the second coming. However, this means they also do not believe in the testimony of Jesus, who died, rose again, and is coming back, because Jesus Himself said, "Behold, I am coming quickly! Blessed is he who keeps the words of the prophecy of this book" (Revelation 22:7).

We can know that a prophecy comes from God if it affirms the second coming of Christ while meeting other biblical tests of authenticity (see, for example, 1 John 4:1–3) and challenges the church to prepare. God is still speaking, and significant portions of what He has foretold in the Bible are yet to be seen and fulfilled.

WHEN WE DO NOT KNOW THE WORD OF GOD, WE HAVE NO BASIS FOR JUDGING PROPHECY.

2. THE HOLY SPIRIT

The Holy Spirit reveals the *"deep things of God"* (1 Corinthians 2:10) and works out the Lord's original intentions. *"However, when He, the Spirit of truth, has come, He will guide you into all truth; for He will not speak on His own authority, but whatever He hears He will speak; and He will tell you things to come"* (John 16:13). The Spirit is revealing the mysteries of the end times now more than ever. I want to emphasize again that without the revelation of the Holy Spirit, we can have no clear guidance about what to do and how to do it. And without the Holy Spirit Himself, we would have no revelation of our destiny in God; rather, it would seem as if everything that happened in our lives and in the world was by pure coincidence.

We need to understand that in our relationship with God, everything begins with "pre." He *predetermined* His plans for the earth, *"declaring the end from the beginning"* (Isaiah 46:10). He *predestined* us *"to be conformed to the image of His Son"* (Romans 8:29). He *preordained* us *"for good works, which God prepared beforehand that we should walk in them"* (Ephesians 2:10). Thus, our destiny is not something that just happens. God predestines everything from the very beginning. *"And to the angel of the church in Philadelphia write, 'These things says He who is holy, He who is true, "He who has the key of David, He who opens and no one shuts, and shuts and no one opens"'"* (Revelation 3:7).

We require the Holy Spirit's revelation to understand our purpose and destiny and walk in it. Only then can we find meaning in what is happening around us. If you are a child of God, whatever you are currently going through is not an accident. It did not occur "just because," without a reason. It is directly related to the purpose God has for you, and it is designed to help you become stronger in Him. Therefore, no matter the circumstance, praise God. As you praise Him, He will work to make it all end well.

3. THE FEASTS OF THE LORD

The feasts of the Lord mentioned in the Bible enable us to recognize true prophecy by showing us God's timetable in the last days. One of the Hebrew words for "feast" is *moed*, which means "an appointment," or "a fixed time or season." This is the word that is translated as *"feasts"* in the first verse of the following passage:

> *These are the feasts of the LORD.... On the fifteenth day of the seventh month, when you have gathered in the fruit of the land, you shall keep the feast of the LORD for seven days; on the first day there shall be a sabbath-rest, and on the eighth day a sabbath-rest. And you shall take for yourselves on the first day the fruit of beautiful trees, branches of palm trees, the boughs of leafy trees, and willows of the brook; and you shall rejoice before the LORD your God for seven days. You shall keep it as a feast to the LORD for seven days in the year. It shall be a statute forever in your generations. You shall celebrate it in the seventh month.* (Leviticus 23:37, 39–41)

Unfortunately, in much of the church, the teaching known as *dispensationalism* has replaced the revelation of the feasts of the Lord as the indicator of God's last-days timetable. Many Christian colleges and universities teach dispensationalism. A "dispensation" has been defined as "a period of time during which man is tested in respect to obedience to some specific revelation of the will of God."[1]

In dispensationalism, Bible interpreters delineate various stages or periods of time (often seven) in God's plan for mankind. It is unclear, however, when these periods begin or end. Therefore, if we adopt this way of thinking, we cannot have adequate knowledge about God's times and seasons. The feasts do provide us with this knowledge. Dispensations are man-made constructs that Bible interpreters developed to try to better understand redemptive history. However, God Himself appointed the feasts of the Lord, and they are therefore precise in revealing times and seasons.

The Jews believe major events in history are marked by the times of the feasts. For example, they commemorate the "birthday of the world," the day of the creation of Adam and Eve, at Rosh Hashanah, which is also the Jewish New Year. God gave the law to Moses at Mount Sinai at the time of Pentecost. The major events in Christ's redemption of humanity are tied to three main feasts: Passover, Pentecost, and Tabernacles. Jesus had to die during the feast of Passover. He could not have died at any other time because He is the sacrificial Lamb given for the sins of the whole world. The outpouring of the Spirit, whom Jesus said the Father would send in His name, occurred at Pentecost. And the feast of Tabernacles is related to Jesus's second coming.

THE FEASTS OF THE LORD REVEAL THE SEASONS OF GOD.

Over the centuries, the enemy has worked in various ways to prevent God's people from recognizing spiritual seasons. He has usurped

---

1. C. I. Scofield, *Scofield Reference Notes (1917 Edition)*, "Genesis 1," https://www.biblestudytools.com/commentaries/scofield-reference-notes/genesis/genesis-1.html.

God's patterns in order to bring confusion. Among other things, he has altered the calendar through which humanity marks time on earth. Daniel anticipated it in this way: *"He shall speak pompous words against the Most High, shall persecute the saints of the Most High, and shall intend to change times and law. Then the saints shall be given into his hand for a time and times and half a time"* (Daniel 7:25). An early Roman lunar calendar is said to have used a ten-month system with 304 days a year. This was a forerunner to the Gregorian solar calendar of twelve months and 365 days a year, which most of the world uses today. The Jewish calendar is lunisolar, while the calendar that governs the Muslim world—either for civic or religious purposes, or both—is solely lunar.

Our current calendar systems may have their everyday uses, but they are not helpful for discerning spiritual seasons or pointing to the prophetic time we are currently in. The feasts of the Lord can enable us to truly understand God's timetable. Not all the feasts have been completely fulfilled, but they will be. God's times have been established for eternity; they do not change. And the feasts reveal His eternal purposes. Without the revelation of these feasts, we will remain blind to those purposes. That is why we must return to recognizing their importance and seeking to understand them.

The feasts are also significant because they are times when portals to the spiritual realm are opened. We can say that heaven draws nearer to earth during these periods, when visitations from God to His people, angelic activity, supernatural protection, miracles, cycles of blessing, and the fulfillment of promises occur. While unusual events in the physical realm may occur at any time, they do not carry the same weight or meaning as they do when they happen during one of the feasts.

As believers, we are called to celebrate these feasts of the Lord. The fact that most Christians are not Jewish by heritage does not exempt us! On the contrary, we are supposed to celebrate the feasts with greater revelation due to the coming of Jesus Christ. The following are the feasts the church should be observing:

- The feast of Passover, which was fulfilled by the death of Christ

- The feast of Pentecost, the beginning of which was fulfilled by the coming of the Holy Spirit, recounted in the book of Acts. This is the feast of the church age. We are still in this feast, although we are moving toward its conclusion.

- The feast of Tabernacles, which, as mentioned earlier, is the feast that will precede the coming of the Lord

God commanded the Jewish people to keep these feasts, which required following certain rituals and traditions. Christians celebrate them not by law or tradition but in the knowledge that they are connected to the purposes of our Lord Jesus Christ. Communion is a common example of a feast of the Lord that Christians celebrate, even though they may not realize it. Many Christians do not know that communion was instituted to recognize the fulfillment of the feast of Passover. We can also celebrate Yom Kippur, or the Day of Atonement, by humbling ourselves and repenting before God. We don't need a high priest to offer an animal sacrifice in the temple every year in order to receive atonement for our sins. Jesus Christ is the eternal High Priest who offered Himself as our sacrifice once for all time. At Yom Kippur, we can set aside a day to acknowledge the tremendous sacrifice Jesus made for us.[2]

WITHOUT AN UNDERSTANDING OF THE FEASTS OF THE LORD, IT IS IMPOSSIBLE TO KNOW WHERE WE ARE ON GOD'S TIMETABLE.

---

2. To read more about new covenant meanings of the feasts of the Lord, see Mark Levit and John J. Parsons, "The Jewish Holidays: A Simplified Overview of the Feasts of the Lord," Hebrew for Christians, https://www.hebrew4christians.com/Holidays/Introduction/introduction.html.

APPLICATIONS OF BIBLICAL PROPHECY

The prophecy in the Bible gives us revelation regarding three groups: Israel, the church, and the world. If we were to exclude any of these three, prophecy would be incomplete. The prophecies for each of these groups are distinct. They have different times, signs, and ways of relating to one another. Let's take a brief look at each area.

ISRAEL

For almost two thousand years prior to twentieth century, the Jewish people were spread to all corners of the earth. However, in 1948, the State of Israel was established. Since then, millions of Jews have returned to the Holy Land to live in a nation situated on their ancient territory. In 1980, the legislative body of Israel declared Jerusalem to be its capital by law. In 2017, we witnessed the jubilee of Jerusalem when the United States officially recognized the holy city as Israel's capital and announced it would move its embassy there. Without Jerusalem, Israel would be incomplete because, when Christ returns, the world will come to Jerusalem to worship Him during the millennium.

The reestablishment of the State of Israel was a phenomenon that had never before occurred in the history of the world: the descendants of a conquered people, scattered across the globe in a Diaspora over thousands of years, gathered in their former homeland and were constituted as a nation once more. Other countries of the world—a majority of the members of the United Nations—voted yes to this reconstitution. Unknowingly, they were voting for the fulfillment of a promise from God. What Ezekiel prophesied in chapters 36–37 of his book has been fulfilled. One passage reads:

> But you, O mountains of Israel, you shall shoot forth your branches and yield your fruit to My people Israel, for they are about to come. For indeed I am for you, and I will turn to you, and you shall be tilled and sown. I will multiply men upon you, all the house of Israel, all of it; and the cities shall be inhabited and the ruins rebuilt. I will multiply upon you man and beast; and they shall increase and bear

young; I will make you inhabited as in former times, and do better for you than at your beginnings. Then you shall know that I am the LORD. *Yes, I will cause men to walk on you, My people Israel; they shall take possession of you, and you shall be their inheritance; no more shall you bereave them of children.* (Ezekiel 36:8–12)

In Matthew 24, Jesus spoke about the fig tree, a symbol of the nation of Israel: "*Now learn this parable from the fig tree: When its branch has already become tender and puts forth leaves, you know that summer is near. So you also, when you see all these things, know that it is near—at the doors!*" (Matthew 24:32–33). Israel is the fig tree and the apple of God's eye. For two thousand years, people had said, "Israel is finished." But then the prophecies were fulfilled, and the nation came back to life. Many preachers cannot explain this phenomenon because they believe in "replacement theology," which says that the church has replaced Israel in God's purposes. This is not true. God has a plan for both Israel and the church. He made covenantal promises to Israel, and those promises are as valid today as they were thousands of years ago.

You and I are living during a period when biblical end-time prophecies about Israel are being fulfilled. Peter, Paul, and the rest of the apostles never saw this day; they could only long for it, dream about it, and declare that it would occur, but they did not witness it as we and other believers in the recent past have. This is the privilege God has given our generation. And there are more prophesies yet to be fulfilled, including ones about the Jews recognizing Jesus as their true Messiah.

THE REBIRTH OF ISRAEL AS A NATION IS ONE OF THE END-TIME PROPHECIES FULFILLED IN THE TWENTIETH CENTURY.

THE CHURCH OF CHRIST

Biblical prophecies about the church include predictions of persecution, apostasy, and the faithfulness of God's remnant. We have seen more prophecies regarding the church fulfilled in the last century than ever before. Some prophecies that have to do with the persecution of the church were fulfilled during the Middle Ages, but others are still being fulfilled today in countries where Christianity is outlawed or ostracized. (See, for example, Matthew 24:9–10.) At the same time, especially in the West, the church is going through one of its biggest times of apostasy, as predicted. (See, for example, 1 Timothy 4:1.) We are seeing a departure from the faith, from the supernatural, and from the ministry of the Holy Spirit that is quite alarming.

The Pew Research Center published a report on the accelerating decline of Christianity in the United States. Telephone surveys conducted between 2018 and 2019 found that 65 percent of American adults define themselves as Christian, which is 12 percent lower than the previous decade. Those with no religious affiliation, who define themselves as "atheist, agnostic, or 'nothing in particular,'" are at 26 percent, compared to the 17 percent reported in 2009.[3]

Meanwhile, significant portions of the church are ignoring or renouncing the supernatural, the power of the Holy Spirit, and the full efficacy of the cross. The church has moved away from the priesthood of believers, prayer, worship, and fasting. Instead, for many congregations, church has become merely a social club. Some may try to help their communities and the world, but they are attempting to do so without the power of the cross and God's Spirit. Apostasy begins when Christians dissociate themselves from the Holy Spirit and the supernatural, and it culminates when they renounce their faith in Jesus Christ.

But there is a remnant of Christians who wholeheartedly embrace the Holy Spirit, the supernatural, and all that God desires to pour out

---

3. "In U.S., Decline of Christianity Continues at Rapid Pace," Pew Research Center, Washington, D.C., October 17, 2019, https://www.pewforum.org/2019/10/17/in-u-s-decline-of-christianity-continues-at-rapid-pace/. (Please see copyright page for disclaimer regarding Pew Research Center data cited throughout this book.)

upon His people. I believe these Christians constitute the true, uncompromised church. We see a reference to this faithful remnant in the book of Revelation, which repeats the phrase *"he who overcomes."* (See, for example, Revelation 2:7; 3:5; 21:7.)

This generation is on the verge of seeing the greatest outpouring of the Holy Spirit and the greatest revival in history. The remnant church is about to enter into the glory of God. This remnant will complete its spiritual cycle when the bride of Christ is taken up by her Bridegroom, Jesus. The earth began with the glory of God manifested in creation, and it will end with the glory manifested in the supernatural wonders of the last days, which God is about to reveal. The movement of the end times will be a sovereign movement of God Himself.

In these days, the Lord wants to reveal Himself more fully to the church, and that is why He is bringing manifestations of His glory. Only when we dwell in His glory will we stop looking to human beings for our strength and help, and look to Him instead. *"But as it is written: 'Eye has not seen, nor ear heard, nor have entered into the heart of man the things which God has prepared for those who love Him.' But God has revealed them to us through His Spirit. For the Spirit searches all things, yes, the deep things of God"* (1 Corinthians 2:9–10). The Holy Spirit is disclosing more spiritual understanding about God's elect than ever before. It is only through the revelation of the Spirit of God that we will see what no eye has seen and hear what no ear has heard!

THE WORLD

End-time prophecies about the world include predictions of widespread confusion and an increase in learning. When Jesus talked about the signs of the end times, He included the sign of *"perplexity"* or bewilderment: *"And there will be signs in the sun, in the moon, and in the stars; and on the earth distress of nations, with perplexity, the sea and the waves roaring"* (Luke 21:25). This means the people of the world will not know what to do about the troubles they experience globally and in their communities.

Furthermore, in the book of Daniel, we read, *"Many shall run to and fro, and knowledge shall increase"* (Daniel 12:4). Since the beginning of the twentieth century, mankind has created airplanes and vehicles that travel in space; invented cell phones and robotics; developed new medicines, vaccines, and surgeries; and much more. Mankind continues to make great advances in science, technology, and medicine. But even with all this acquired knowledge, human beings are confounded by dire issues for which there seem to be no answers. The world is perplexed by problems such as natural disasters; environmental distress; diseases, illnesses, and plagues; corrupt governments; divisive politics; and economic unpredictability. Additionally, people are worried about ongoing security issues, such as political instability in the Middle East and the threat of terrorist attacks.

Individuals also struggle with perplexity in their personal lives. Are you facing perplexity in your finances? Marriage? Family? Health? Are you about to lose everything? Do you feel cornered, with no way out? There is always a way out with God! Just because you can't discern Him working right now doesn't mean He isn't aware of your needs. It simply means He hasn't yet revealed His answers or you haven't yet discerned them. The Holy Spirit can reveal these answers to you. God has solutions for all our concerns. We must learn to listen and hear what He is saying to us.

REVELATION IS THE WAY OUT OF ALL PERPLEXITY. WHEN THE REVELATION COMES, THE CONFUSION ENDS.

Why has God allowed a spirit of confusion to operate on earth amid all our advanced human knowledge? It is because human beings must understand that, without God, His Word, and His Spirit, we cannot find the answers to the great problems confronting our generation.

Governmental leaders, scientists, bankers, celebrities, athletes, doctors, and lawyers will increasingly face bewilderment but experience no relief. They will desperately desire answers but find none.

I have concluded that the only time people become serious with God is when they are going through a crisis. Our world is clearly facing the types of crises for which there is no way out, humanly speaking. Only God has the answers. Just as the solutions to our individual problems will come by revelation from God's Spirit, the answers to humanity's perplexities will come by revelation.

As a church, we must be ready to receive and pass along God's revelation to resolve these perplexities. In order to do this, we must return to the basics of truth, faith, the supernatural, the cross, the resurrection, the power of God, the blood of Christ, and other potent spiritual realities God has revealed in His Word. This is the only way we can stand firm as the faithful remnant, ministering to the world while preparing the way for the second coming of Christ.

> *And the Spirit and the bride say, "Come!" And let him who hears say, "Come!"* (Revelation 22:17)

Maranatha! Jesus Christ is coming soon!

SUMMARY

+ The Holy Spirit is calling and gathering the remnant in the church; this remnant will prepare the way for the second coming of the Lord.

+ The church today has a deficiency of revealed knowledge and prophecy; the enemy has been stealing this revelation from God's people throughout the centuries, seeking to generate confusion and unbelief.

+ We can only recognize spiritual times and seasons through the revelation of God's Spirit and prophecy—including the prophetic aspects of the feasts of the Lord.

+ Our *fundamental* spiritual knowledge comes from the teachings and examples in the Scriptures, or the written Word of God. *Revelational* knowledge comes from *rhemas* of the Holy Spirit, or God's words for us today, for specific situations. The purpose of revealed knowledge is to open our spiritual eyes and understanding so we are aware of the truths and information God desires to give us in the now. *Prophetic* knowledge refers to the prophecy contained in the Bible. The Scriptures tell us that *"the testimony of Jesus is the spirit of prophecy"* (Revelation 19:10). Prophecy enables us to anticipate the future so that we are prepared.

+ God's will is to make His purposes and work known to us in the now and for the future.

+ The prophets of the Old Testament prepared the way for Christ's first coming, and the apostles and prophets of the church will prepare the way for His second coming.

+ Three indisputable bases for recognizing a true prophetic word are the Scriptures, the Holy Spirit, and the feasts of the Lord, which are God's patterns for revealing His eternal plans.

+ The feasts the church must keep are the following: the feast of Passover, which was fulfilled by the death of Christ; the feast of Pentecost, which encompasses the coming of the Holy Spirit and the church age; and the feast of Tabernacles, which is the feast that will precede the coming of the Lord.

+ The prophecy in the Bible gives us revelation regarding three groups: Israel, the church, and the world. If we were to exclude any of these three, prophecy would be incomplete. The prophecies for each of these groups are distinct. They have different times, signs, and ways of relating to one another.

+ A significant prophecy that was fulfilled in the twentieth century was the reconstitution of Israel as a nation, with the establishment of Jerusalem as its capital.

+ Only the revealed knowledge of God can give us a way out of the dire situations in our world that are currently reigning over our times and generating perplexity in the lives of nations, communities, and individuals.

+ *"The Spirit and the bride say, 'Come!'"* (Revelation 22:17).

ACTIVATION

Dear reader, I would like to guide you in praying that the Holy Spirit would begin to reveal to you the urgency of the times in which we live and the nearness of Christ's coming for His church. You need to be prepared, watching and praying with your spiritual eyes open, and in God's perfect will for your life during these momentous days.

Heavenly Father, I thank You for Your written Word, Your Holy Spirit, the prophecy and the prophets that announce Your coming, and the apostles who prepare the people to receive the King of Kings. I ask You to forgive me for not believing in Jesus's second coming, for not seeing the signs, and for thinking that prophecy somehow relates only to others and not to me. Today, I ask You to bring a new revelation into my life and instill in me the urgency of the times in which I am living. I commit to seeking Your presence and listening to the voice of the Holy Spirit.

I want to receive the revelation of the season my generation is currently going through. I want to know what Your will is for me as part of the remnant that awaits the imminent coming of Your Son. I declare a new season in my life and in my relationship with You—a season of revelation, supernatural power, and kingdom advancement in my family, work, church, city, and nation, in Jesus's name! I join my voice with the cry of the Holy Spirit, saying, "Come, Lord Jesus!"

SIGNS OF THE TIMES TESTIMONIES

"REVIVAL HAS COME TO INDIA"

Pastor Anish Mano Stephen is from Bangalore (officially known as Bengaluru) in southern India. A computer engineer by profession, he has been called by God to impact his nation with supernatural power. Today, he is living out his spiritual season with amazing signs under the guidance of the Holy Spirit. Thousands of people who had never before heard of Christ have come to Jesus and seen His miracles and supernatural works. These extraordinary results are part of the fulfillment of God's promise that before the coming of the Lord, the whole world will hear the gospel of salvation.

In 2014, I was a computer engineer for a multinational company, while also pastoring a church in South India, when the Lord called me to full-time ministry. That year, Pastor Chandy, who has a megachurch in New Delhi, took me to Apostle Maldonado's conference in Mumbai on India's west coast. Our church had been moving somewhat in the supernatural, seeing basic healings and small transformations, but nothing compared to what you see in Apostle Maldonado's ministry.

In 2016, we attended the apostle's conference again. While we were there, he invited a small group of pastors, which included me, to a special session. He ministered to us under a great move of the Holy Spirit. Then, he said, "If you believe, this Sunday, you will see the glory of God," and he blessed our building projects and other matters. This was the most powerful word I'd ever received. That Sunday, I went to church and let the Holy Spirit flow without subjecting Him to our agenda. As a result, a spontaneous worship arose. The people were filled with the Spirit and fell at the Lord's feet. This was the first time we had ever experienced something like this, so I asked for testimonies.

While people were testifying, I began to hear a sound like a hailstorm, but when I looked out the window, it wasn't even raining. Then, it felt like the building was shaking, as if an earthquake were occurring. After the tremor passed, I immediately felt an explosion, like that from a small bomb. This caused a tessera, or mosaic tile, to pop out of place from a wall. However, it came out cleanly, without cracking or breaking. All our attention was drawn to that tile. After a pause, I sensed a huge person walking from the tile to the platform and then *right inside me.* Following this, all the tiles came loose, one by one, but there was a great calm and peace in the air. I was praising God for having saved us from the earthquake, but later we realized there had been no earthquake because there was no broken glass, nor was there any destruction outside.

Building security came in, and when they saw what had happened, they said, "Pastor, you have done black magic." I thought, "If they are so quick to believe in the supernatural power of darkness, how can I not believe in the supernatural power of God?" Suddenly, a sister in the church reminded me of Revelation 11:19: *"Then the temple of God was opened in heaven, and the ark of His covenant was seen in His temple. And there were lightnings, noises, thunderings, an earthquake, and great hail."* Civil engineers also came to look at the tiles and said that what had happened was not naturally possible.

After this, many things changed in our ministry. The first was that my faith to believe in the supernatural power of God grew. The news of what had happened spread around the city, and people began to invite me to preach and manifest this same power in other churches. This connected us with the leading pastors of India. Second, my ministry in the north of the country increased. The attendance at crusades grew to up to twenty-five hundred people. People came in ambulances and on stretchers, and God healed them. Areas were transformed where previously there had not been a single believer and the manifestation of miracles and healings was unheard of. Third, the Lord has taken me from making only one mission trip a year to visiting nineteen nations! In 2018, the Lord sent me to Africa for the first time, and we now host crusades in the nations of East Africa.

I am grateful to God for sending Apostle Maldonado to India. I believe that the pastors' meeting we attended opened the heavens over our nation. The powers of darkness were broken, and the pastors and other believers in the country were activated. Although we are facing persecution, revival has come to India and is advancing by huge leaps.

A POWERFUL SUPERNATURAL SEASON

Pastor Pablo Cano of Mexico has seen the manifestation of God in his life because he has entered the season of the remnant that is meant to prepare for the coming of the Lord with supernatural signs. His ministry has multiplied and all kinds of miracles have occurred.

We have been transformed in this season, which began after we connected with King Jesus Ministry. We had originally come to the ministry with an orphan mentality, begging for blessings. After we received the revelation that we are God's children, everything accelerated. In fifteen years, our church had not grown past two hundred people. However, last year, we increased to more than two thousand people, and we haven't stopped growing. Four years ago, we were bringing in a very small tithe, but it is now twenty times greater.

God has given us more than fifteen acres of land in different parts of the city of Puebla, which is southeast of Mexico City. This was without cost to us; all the land was donated! Now, we are also building churches on a mountain in another area an hour and a half from Puebla. Previously, we were holding three to four services a day, but even then, we outgrew our facility. Now, we have a hall that seats more than fifteen hundred people. Everything is accelerating, growing, and multiplying!

In addition, we are seeing many miracles that we had never experienced before, such as creative miracles and people being healed of cancer. A member of our congregation is a street vendor. One day, while she was working, she saw that a man nearby had died. When she asked what had happened, she was told that he had choked on something he had eaten and suffocated. He had been there for an hour. A nurse had certified that he was not breathing and had no pulse. The woman went over and asked to be allowed through to see him. When they said, "Who are you?" she replied, "I am a child of God." Right there, she declared the power of the resurrection, and in a few moments, the man breathed again and stood up! This man was shocked at what had happened to him. The news crew of the most popular radio station in Puebla soon arrived, and the whole city heard the news. All Puebla knew that a woman had prayed in the name of Jesus for a dead man and that he had risen!

CHAPTER 2

THE FULLNESS OF THE TIMES

Solomon was Israel's greatest king and the son of the celebrated King David. He built the temple that his father had dreamed of constructing, so that God could be honored and His presence dwell in the Holy of Holies. Solomon was also a prolific writer and left behind many proverbs of wisdom. However, he never reached the same level of revelation his father had concerning the coming Messiah, Jesus Christ. (See, for example, Psalm 22.) That is why, with regard to times and seasons, Solomon wrote the following:

> *To everything there is a season, a time for every purpose under heaven: a time to be born, and a time to die; a time to plant, and a time to pluck what is planted; a time to kill, and a time to heal; a time to break down, and a time to build up; a time to weep, and a time to laugh; a time to mourn, and a time to dance; a time to cast away stones, and a time to gather stones; a time to embrace, and a time to refrain from embracing; a time to gain, and a time to lose; a time to keep, and a time to throw away; a time to tear, and a time to*

sew; a time to keep silence, and a time to speak.

(Ecclesiastes 3:1–7)

In this passage, Solomon describes the cycles, times, and seasons on earth under natural conditions. I sense that his life was full of ups and downs and he was unfulfilled. Essentially, his conclusion was that, in life, sometimes we win and sometimes we lose. We need to put his statements into the proper context, remembering that he wrote them before Christ came to earth, died on the cross to redeem us, and rose again to give us true life. Solomon lived under the old covenant, and he was not born again. As previously mentioned, unlike his father, who was a "man after God's own heart" (see 1 Samuel 13:14; Acts 13:22), he had not received a revelation of the coming Messiah. Despite the fact that, in his day, Solomon was the richest man who had ever lived, he never achieved an abundant life. In the New Testament, he is not even mentioned among the heroes of the faith.

When we are in Christ, we are not limited by earthly cycles, times, and seasons. Even if we have strayed from God's purposes, He is able to restore or activate spiritual seasons in our lives, bringing us back into line with His will so we can serve Him wholeheartedly and bring Him glory.

WHAT IS THE "FULLNESS OF THE TIMES"?

God is a God of supernatural cycles, times, and seasons, which He determines. A *cycle* is a period of time that has a beginning and an end point. A *season* is a period of time marked by supernatural favor. God's appointed times are different from time on earth as we experience it day to day and year to year. As we have noted, earthly time is imprecise for marking God's movements in history. This is because time as we know it, with the limitations it places on us, is an aspect of the fall, part of the consequences for mankind's sin in the garden of Eden.

We human beings experience God's cycles and seasons within our earthly realm and its time strictures. Nevertheless, because they are supernatural and eternal, they transcend time. This is another reason why, as we discussed in chapter 1, the feasts of the Lord are more precise than dispensationalism for determining God's timetable. Dispensationalism is based on human time frames, while the feasts are based on God's seasons.

> **WE ARE NOW LIVING IN A FULLNESS OF TIME WHEN EVERYTHING IS BECOMING ALIGNED WITH THE IMMINENCE OF CHRIST'S SECOND COMING.**

In addition to spiritual cycles, times, and seasons, there is the "fullness of the times":

*Blessed be the God and Father of our Lord Jesus Christ, who has blessed us with every spiritual blessing in the heavenly places in Christ, just as He chose us in Him before the foundation of the world, that we should be holy and without blame before Him in love, having predestined us to adoption as sons by Jesus Christ to Himself, according to the good pleasure of His will,...having made known to us the mystery of His will, according to His good pleasure which He purposed in Himself, that in the dispensation of **the fullness of the times** He might gather together in one all things in Christ, both which are in heaven and which are on earth—in Him.*

(Ephesians 1:3–5, 9–10)

Prophetically, a fullness of time represents maturity, perfection, reconciliation, consolidation, full growth, and the time of fulfillment. It is the climax or high point of a cycle. The "*fullness of the times*" mentioned in the first chapter of Ephesians refers to the end of an ordered period of time or cycle that God has purposed. He formulated this cycle in accordance with the completeness of His own being. The "*fullness of the times*" speaks of all things coming together in Christ at the end of all time:

> *Having made known to us the mystery of His will, according to His good pleasure which He purposed in Himself, that in the dispensation of the fullness of the times He might gather together in one all things in Christ, both which are in heaven and which are on earth—in Him.* (Ephesians 1:9–10)

THE FULLNESS OF THE TIMES IS NOT ACCOMPLISHED BY OUR FAITH; IT IS A SOVEREIGN ACT OF COMPLETION BY GOD.

The fullness of our times will be manifested at the completion of God's megacycle. I refer to this cycle as "mega" because there will be a convergence of the first glory with the final glory, the natural with the spiritual. (See Haggai 2:6–9.) Recently, you may have noticed that many aspects of life appear to have accelerated. The hours of the day, the months, and even the years seem to pass more quickly than before. This is even happening in the physical realm. NASA says that changes in atmospheric winds and oceanic currents, as well as earthquakes, may be responsible for literally shortening our days in a minute way. For example, the earthquake that occurred in Japan in March 2011 likely shifted the earth's figure axis more than six inches and made the planet spin a little faster.[4]

I believe that because we are approaching the fulfillment of God's megacycle, we are experiencing a spiritual acceleration that is affecting

---

4. Alan Buis, "Japan Quake May Have Shortened Earth Days, Moved Axis," NASA, March 14, 2011, https://www.nasa.gov/topics/earth/features/japanquake/earth20110314.html. The figure axis is "the axis about which Earth's mass is balanced...not [to] be confused with its north-south axis."

the natural world. This acceleration has also hastened the appearance of the signs of the end times. In many cases, what wasn't expected to occur for another few centuries has happened in a matter of a few generations.

All fulfillment requires alignment with heaven. The fullness of the times is the means by which God's purposes for the world will accumulate to an apex. At its peak, this fullness will bring about the fulfillment of all remaining prophecies. Fullness is progressive, cumulative, and generational. A certain generation may be privileged to see the accumulation reach its fullness, but the fullness has been gestated throughout many preceding generations.

> **WE ARE APPROACHING THE COMPLETION OF GOD'S MEGACYCLE BECAUSE WE ARE NEAR TO THE FULLNESS OF ALL THINGS, WHERE TIME WILL HAVE REACHED ITS PEAK.**

As far as the church is concerned, there is a difference between the fullness of the times and the end of an era. The fullness of the times is the completion of *all* things, whereas the end of an era is the completion of one aspect of God's purposes. Not all endings of an era look the same, but what is common to all is that they signal the conclusion of something old and the birth of something new. If something new does not manifest, it is safe to say we are still in the same era. For example, after Jesus came, John the Baptist left; thus, the end of John's assignment marked the beginning of Jesus's ministry. Jesus and John were contemporaries, having been born months apart. However, their ministries were for different times. John's mission closed the old covenant, while Jesus's mission opened the new covenant.

With fullness, there are different levels and measures of completeness. Even the second coming of Christ at the beginning of the millennial age concerns the fullness of an era or of *a* time, but not of *all* times. This is why it is so important for us to understand the fullness of the times.

THE EVENTS THAT WILL MARK THE END OF THIS AGE ARE THE RAPTURE OF THE CHURCH AND THE SECOND COMING OF CHRIST.

Let us consider various events for which there was a fullness of time. God fashioned the earth during a spiritual feast in which all aspects of creation were made complete and fully mature. (See Genesis 2:1–3.) It was the fullness of a time because it was the end of one era and the beginning of another as God began a relationship with the human beings He had created. Jesus was born in the fullness of a time—the time of the law under the old covenant. *"When the fullness of the time had come, God sent forth His Son, born of a woman, born under the law"* (Galatians 4:4). The church was born in the fullness of a time during the feast of Pentecost. We know the church was not birthed randomly because Jesus had been very specific about it with His disciples before He ascended to the Father's throne. He told the disciples they should wait for the time to be fulfilled and the Holy Spirit to be sent to them in His place. (See Luke 24:49.) Jesus will come back for His bride in the fullness of a time that marks the end of the church era. (See 1 Thessalonians 4:15–17.) And, as mentioned previously, Jesus will return to earth to begin His millennial reign in the fullness of a time at the end of the great tribulation; then, the world will begin a new, thousand-year era in which all nations will worship Christ as King.

WHAT IS FULLNESS BASED ON?

How can we recognize the fullness of a time? Fullness is based on two very marked events: the manifestation and the harvest. Let's look at each of these elements separately.

THE MANIFESTATION

We cannot define the harvest without first defining the manifestation. We are about to see the greatest harvest of souls for the kingdom that has ever been reaped. But first we will witness the manifestation of divine promises, dreams, visions, prophecies, miracles, signs, wonders, and resources that have not yet been fulfilled for the people of God. Remember, as God's megacycle culminates, there will be a confluence of the first glory and the final glory, in fulfillment of His Word: *"I will give you the rain for your land in its season, the early rain and the latter rain, that you may gather in your grain, your new wine, and your oil"* (Deuteronomy 11:14).

THE STRENGTH OF THE MANIFESTATION IS BASED UPON THE MATURITY OF THE TIMES AND PEOPLE'S CHARACTER IN CHRIST.

THE HARVEST

The harvest is the climax of spiritual accumulation, where we see the ripeness, or fullness, of the fruit. This will happen at the same time the manifestation occurs. Several of the feasts in the Old Testament occur around harvesttime. *"Jesus said to [His disciples], 'My food is to do the will of Him who sent Me, and to finish His work. Do you not say, "There are still four months and then comes the harvest"? Behold, I say to you, lift up your eyes and look at the fields, for they are already white for harvest!'"*

(John 4:34–35). Here Jesus speaks about a spiritual harvest, saying that the fruit has already ripened and manifested for the kingdom of God.

However, we must understand that the fruit of the last harvest will be both good and bad. As I explain in the next section, now is the time when we will harvest whatever seeds we have sown in our life. We must make sure that we are right with God.

We can see that the harvest from seeds sown for the gospel over many years is being reaped and will continue to be reaped. According to a survey conducted by the Pew Research Center in eighteen countries in Latin America and Puerto Rico, the number of Protestants in these nations has grown exponentially since the beginning of the twentieth century. "Nearly one-in-five Latin Americans now describe themselves as Protestant, and across the countries surveyed majorities of them self-identify as Pentecostal or belong to a Pentecostal denomination...with an emphasis on the 'gifts of the Holy Spirit,' such as speaking in tongues, faith healing and prophesying."[5] In Africa, Christianity has grown from ten million in 1900, to one hundred and forty-four million in 1970, to more than four hundred million at the beginning of the twenty-first century. That is 46 percent of the population.[6] The harvest is ready!

FOUR TYPES OF FULLNESS

Let us now look at four types of fullness that we will either experience or witness in our times.

1. THE FULLNESS OF BIRTH

With a physical pregnancy, the "fullness of time" that signals the maturity of gestation is nine months. A pregnancy that reaches full term produces a wholly developed child. If a baby is born before that

---

5. David Masci, "Why Has Pentecostalism Grown So Dramatically in Latin America?" Fact Tank: News in the Numbers, Pew Research Center, Washington, D.C., November 14, 2014, https://www.pewresearch.org/fact-tank/2014/11/14/why-has-pentecostalism-grown-so-dramatically-in-latin-america/.

6 "Overview: Pentecostalism in Africa," *Spirit and Power: A 10-Country Survey of Pentecostals*, Pew Research Center, Washington, D.C., October 5, 2006, https://www.pewforum.org/2006/10/05/overview-pentecostalism-in-africa/.

time, it is considered premature because it has not completed its cycle of growth. Depending on how early the baby arrives, it may need to receive special medical treatment so that its body, including its internal organs, can continue to develop until it can function safely on its own. Without this treatment, the baby might die or suffer physical problems.

Similarly, some Christians have not yet reached maturity and may be in spiritual danger. It is as if they are premature babies and require special attention and care to grow strong in their faith and in the knowledge of Christ. In such cases, spiritual leaders and other believers must pray for and guide them until Jesus is formed within them. *"My little children, for whom I labor in birth again until Christ is formed in you"* (Galatians 4:19). It is especially vital in these last days for believers to develop spiritual maturity so they will be able to stand strong during intense persecution and other attacks of the enemy.

Today, God is in the process of giving birth to something new in the world because the time of gestation for our current age is nearly completed. When Jesus died on the cross and was resurrected, He fulfilled all that He came to earth to accomplish during that period. Then, at Pentecost, Jesus gave birth to the church, which would manifest His new covenant in the world. Now, we are nearing the fullness of all matters concerning the second coming of Christ so that God's ultimate purposes can be birthed.

2. THE FULLNESS OF CHARACTER

The fullness of character is the aspect of God's megacycle in which He is bringing the body of Christ to maturity. *"And He Himself gave some to be apostles, some prophets, some evangelists, and some pastors and teachers, for the equipping of the saints for the work of ministry, for the edifying of the body of Christ"* (Ephesians 4:11–12).

The fullness of our times is represented by two "cups"—one of iniquity and one of mercy. When the cup of iniquity is filled, the wrath of God will be unleashed on the world. Only those who have contributed to filling the cup of mercy will be saved.

At this time, we will see people's character manifested in its fullness before our eyes, whether their character is good or evil. On the good side, we will see the character of Christ come to completeness within believers. On the evil side, we will see iniquity reach its fullest expression within people in the world; in other words, evil men will become much more evil. *"He who is unjust, let him be unjust still; he who is filthy, let him be filthy still; he who is righteous, let him be righteous still; he who is holy, let him be holy still"* (Revelation 22:11).

The increase of evil in our world is obvious. A United Nations report states that violence has intensified, and armed conflicts have become more lethal. However, crime kills more people than armed conflict and terrorism combined. In 2017, while armed conflict claimed 89,000 lives and terrorism claimed 26,000, crime reigned supreme, claiming a total of 464,000 lives.[7]

Thus, we are living in dangerous times in which we will see the corruption of people's character firsthand. Again, whatever is debased and evil will become even more so. Paul warned his disciple Timothy,

> But know this, that in the last days perilous times will come: For men will be lovers of themselves, lovers of money, boasters, proud, blasphemers, disobedient to parents, unthankful, unholy, unloving, unforgiving, slanderers, without self-control, brutal, despisers of good, traitors, headstrong, haughty, lovers of pleasure rather than lovers of God, having a form of godliness but denying its power. And from such people turn away! (2 Timothy 3:1–5)

Once more, I warn you that we can expect to experience the progression of who we are today, whether it is good or evil. If you are doing wrong in the eyes of God and continue to rebel against Him, refusing to repent and change, you will get worse. If you are in a state of rebellion, it is because you do not hear God; your heart has become hardened and no longer yields to the conviction of the Holy Spirit. However, the Lord

---

7. Joanne Lu, "Countries with the Highest Murder Rates, Ranked in a New UN Report," *UN Dispatch*, July 12, 2019, https://www.undispatch.com/countries-with-the-highest-murder-rates-ranked-in-a-new-un-report/.

is working on the character of His remnant bride to make her *"holy and without blemish"*:

> *That He might sanctify and cleanse her with the washing of water by the word, that He might present her to Himself a glorious church, not having spot or wrinkle or any such thing, but that she should be holy and without blemish.* (Ephesians 5:26–27)

The church and individual believers will experience spiritual cleansing to build up their character and enable them to come to spiritual maturity. Will you yield to the Holy Spirit today and allow Him to purify you?

3. THE FULLNESS OF TIME

As noted, the *"fullness of the times"* refers to the gathering or completion of all things in Christ: *"That in the dispensation of the fullness of the times He might gather together in one all things in Christ, both which are in heaven and which are on earth—in Him"* (Ephesians 1:10). Likewise, with the fullness of times in which we are living, we will see the manifestation of the maturity of our character, anointing, faith, power, and ministry, which have been accumulating. The fullness is preceded by the character-development process, which sustains us and leads us to be part of God's remnant during the manifestation and harvest.

Signs that mark the fullness of our times include the blood moon and the culmination of the feast of Pentecost, the completion of the church age. Let's first examine the sign of the blood moon.

THE SIGN OF THE BLOOD MOON

> *I will show wonders in heaven above and signs in the earth beneath: blood and fire and vapor of smoke. The sun shall be turned into darkness, and the moon into blood, before the coming of the great and awesome day of the LORD.* (Acts 2:19–20)

Not only does the blood moon represent a fullness of time, but it also represents the end of an era by pointing to the coming of the Lord in the rapture. In the last two thousand years, there have been fifty-six tetrads of blood moons, with eight of them occurring during feasts of the Lord.[8] What exactly is a tetrad? This term generally refers to a group of four things. In this case, it is used to designate four total lunar eclipses within two consecutive years, with no partial lunar eclipses in between.[9] For example, there was a blood moon on April 15, 2014, during the feast of Passover. There was another on October 8 of the same year during the feast of Tabernacles. Two more blood moons occurred in the year 2015, on April 4 during Passover and on September 28 during Tabernacles.[10]

These four blood moons represent the four ends of the earth. Their appearance tells us that a calamity of global proportions is about to happen. In fact, it has already begun. The entire world will undergo terrible dilemmas—failing economies, natural disasters, violent confrontations, health emergencies, and widespread death. It is not just individual nations that will struggle with these distressing conditions. All nations will deal with such emergencies on a large scale. Because of global connectedness, many of these predicaments will affect multiple nations and even the whole earth. As mentioned earlier, no leader or government will be able to find solutions to these unprecedented situations.

In the last seventy years, there have been five blood-moon tetrads,[11] although only three have occurred during feasts. The phenomenon in which a blood moon coincides with a feast is not set to happen again for another 549 years.[12] However, we should remember that supernatural events will occur even outside of the feast times.

8. John Henry, "Eight Tetrads Since the Day of Christ Falling on the First and Last of the Seven Feasts of the Lord," Landmark Bible Baptist Net, April 15, 2014, http://prophecy.landmarkbiblebaptist.net/Signs/8Tetrads.html.
9. Aparna Kher, "What Is a Blood Moon?" Time and Date AS, https://www.timeanddate.com/eclipse/blood-moon.html, and Bruce McClure and Deborah Byrd, "What's a Blood Moon?" EarthSky, July 15, 2019, https://earthsky.org/human-world/what-is-a-blood-moon-lunar-eclipses-2014-2015.
10. McClure and Byrd, "What's a Blood Moon?"
11. "Lunar Eclipses: 1901 to 2000," NASA Eclipse Web Site, https://eclipse.gsfc.nasa.gov/LEcat5/LE1901-2000.html, and "Lunar Eclipses: 2001 to 2100," NASA Eclipse Web Site, https://eclipse.gsfc.nasa.gov/LEcat5/LE2001-2100.html.
12. Henry, "Eight Tetrads Since the Day of Christ."

Most scientists consider blood moons to be merely natural phenomena. However, in our day, there is more to them than that. For the first time in over two thousand years, the Hebrew and the Gregorian calendars—the spiritual and the natural—have been aligned. The most recent blood-moon tetrad (in 2015) fell on Passover and the feast of Tabernacles. This sign indicates that we are entering the last portion of the season before the second coming. It is confirmation from God about Jesus's return. Scientists can tell us what a blood moon is, but they don't know what it points to. The Holy Spirit is the only One who can reveal and interpret this sign.

> **THE BLOOD MOON IS A SIGN THAT POINTS TO THE END OF AN ERA, THE FULLNESS OF A TIME, AND THE COMING OF THE LORD.**

THE SIGN OF THE FEAST OF PENTECOST

Another sign of fullness in our times is the culmination of the feast of Pentecost, also known as the feast of Harvest. Again, this feast represents the age of the Holy Spirit, of His outpouring and anointing on the earth. The book of Acts gives this account of the Spirit's coming:

When the Day of Pentecost had fully come, [the followers of Jesus] were all with one accord in one place. And suddenly there came a sound from heaven, as of a rushing mighty wind, and it filled the whole house where they were sitting. Then there appeared to them divided tongues, as of fire, and one sat upon each of them. And they were all filled with the Holy Spirit and began to speak with other tongues, as the Spirit gave them utterance. (Acts 2:1–4)

Thus began the era of the church. The moment the Spirit came, the spiritual feast of Pentecost was initiated. As mentioned previously, this feast continues to the present day. We are now in the last part of it. The Jewish feast of Pentecost is celebrated over a period of two days. In relation to the era of the church, this period signifies two thousand years. Keep in mind that, for the Lord, one day is equivalent to a thousand years: *"But, beloved, do not forget this one thing, that with the Lord one day is as a thousand years, and a thousand years as one day"* (2 Peter 3:8).

It has been more than two thousand years since Jesus was born, but it has been less than two thousand years since the spiritual feast of Pentecost began. According to God's timetable, Christ will return at the end of the feast of Pentecost, or after two thousand years. *"After two days He will revive us; on the third day He will raise us up, that we may live in His sight"* (Hosea 6:2).

Most scholars now estimate that Jesus was born in the year 4 BC. An error was made in the original calculation of years that determined the date Christ was born, which delineated when "BC" ended and "AD" began. Jesus died and rose again at the age of thirty-three. Using the original calculation, the year of Jesus's resurrection would have been AD 33. In that case, only 1,987 years have passed. If we use the revised calculation, which is adjusted four years, 1,991 years have gone by. Either way, we have not yet reached the two-thousand-year mark for the end of the Passover feast.

As I explained in chapter 1, over the centuries, the enemy has worked in various ways to prevent God's people from recognizing His spiritual seasons by altering the calendar by which mankind measures time. The Bible is clear that no one knows the day or hour of Christ's return. Jesus said, *"But of that day and hour no one knows, not even the angels of heaven, but My Father only"* (Matthew 24:36). However, this does not mean we cannot recognize the *season* in which He will return. Again, the feasts mark the seasons of God. Paul wrote, *"But concerning the times and the seasons, brethren, you have no need that I should write to you. For you yourselves know perfectly that the day of the Lord so comes as a thief in the night"* (1 Thessalonians 5:1–2).

Thus, anyone who tells you they know the exact day and hour when Jesus will return is either in great error or lying. Yet we can become familiar with the cycle, the times, and the season in which His coming will occur. I believe all indications are here. Therefore, we must remain in expectation of the greatest outpouring of the Holy Spirit, miracles, signs, and wonders that the earth has ever seen. We also need to be attentive to what is happening with regard to Israel, the church, and the world. In each of these groups, events will accumulate, leading to the manifestation of God's glory.

I can say with great certainty, based on the Word of God, the Holy Spirit, and the feasts, that we are the generation that will see the return of the Lord. Why? Because although there are some significant biblical prophecies still to be completed, most of the prophecies and signs have already been fulfilled. Christ may appear this very decade or the beginning of the next. His coming is imminent. Are you prepared? Are you part of the remnant, the bride of Christ? *"He who testifies to these things says, 'Surely I am coming quickly.' Amen. Even so, come, Lord Jesus!"* (Revelation 22:20).

4. THE FULLNESS OF HARVEST

As the fullness of the times unfolds, we will see two separate harvests: the harvest of mercy toward the church and the harvest of judgment toward the world.

> *Then I looked, and behold, a white cloud, and on the cloud sat One like the Son of Man, having on His head a golden crown, and in His hand a sharp sickle. And another angel came out of the temple, crying with a loud voice to Him who sat on the cloud, "Thrust in Your sickle and reap, for the time has come for You to reap, for the harvest of the earth is ripe." So, He who sat on the cloud thrust in His sickle on the earth, and the earth was reaped.*
>
> (Revelation 14:14–16)

To review, here is the order in which the fullness of harvest will occur:

First, the early and latter rain will come together, with the outpouring of the Holy Spirit.

And it shall be that if you earnestly obey My commandments which I command you today, to love the LORD your God and serve Him with all your heart and with all your soul, then I will give you the rain for your land in its season, the early rain and the latter rain, that you may gather in your grain, your new wine, and your oil.

(Deuteronomy 11:13–14)

Second, the harvest of souls will be gathered.

After this, the Lord will appear in the rapture to carry away His bride. On earth, this event will be followed by the distress of the great tribulation. The ultimate judgment of the world will come after the millennial period.

OUR GREATEST PURPOSE

As noted at the beginning of this chapter, King Solomon seemed to have had no revelation of the first coming of Jesus and His sacrifice on the cross. Even with all his wisdom, he could not discern what his father, David, had received by inspiration of the Holy Spirit. Solomon's experiences led him to believe that life consists of random ups and downs. He failed to understand that there are divine seasons that affect the affairs of humanity and direct the lives of individuals who live according to God's will.

When Jesus came, He restored our understanding of spiritual cycles, times, and seasons. He realigned us with God's will and gave us spiritual sight to discern the fullness of times. We have the sure hope that even the negative situations we face can be turned to good by the work of the Holy Spirit in our lives. (See Romans 8:28.) We do not only live by natural cycles and times, but also by spiritual seasons that lead us to fulfill our God-given purposes on this earth. And the great purpose we all share is to prepare the way for the coming of the Lord.

We are very close to that event! We cannot remain spiritually asleep. Let me repeat: we must watch and pray, staying in communion with the Holy Spirit, so we can be part of the remnant that cries, "Come, Lord Jesus!"

SUMMARY

+ We are now living in a fullness of time when everything is becoming aligned with the imminence of Christ's second coming.

+ A cycle is a period of time that has a beginning and an end point.

+ A season is a period of time marked by supernatural favor.

+ Time as we know it, with the limitations it places on us, is an aspect of the fall, part of the consequences for mankind's sin in the garden of Eden.

+ The *"fullness of the times"* mentioned in Ephesians 1 refers to the end of an ordered period of time or cycle that God has purposed.

+ The fullness of the times is not accomplished by our faith; it is a sovereign act of completion by God.

+ The fullness of our times will be manifested at the completion of God's megacycle, where there will be a convergence of the first glory with the final glory, the natural with the spiritual.

+ There is a difference between the fullness of the times and the end of an era. The fullness of the times is the completion of *all* things, whereas the end of an era is the completion of one aspect of God's purposes.

+ The second coming of Christ at the beginning of the millennial age concerns the fullness of an era or of *a* time, but not of *all* times.

+ Fullness is based on two very marked events: manifestation and harvest. The manifestation of God's promises will be accompanied by the harvest—the climax of spiritual accumulation—where we will see the ripeness, or fullness, of the fruit.

+ There are four types of fullness: fullness of birth, fullness of character, fullness of time, and fullness of harvest.

+ Signs that mark the fullness of our times include the occurrence of blood moons on feast days and the completion of the spiritual feast of Pentecost.

- No one can know the day or hour when Christ will come, yet we can become familiar with the cycle, the times, and the season in which His coming will occur.

- We are the generation that will see the return of the Lord!

ACTIVATION

The end-time spiritual harvest is ready. The manifestations of the fullness of birth, character, time, and harvest have already begun. We are part of the remnant that will meet Christ at His appearing. This is the end of the "age of grace," in which people have an opportunity to receive salvation in Jesus. Therefore, there is an urgent need to call the nations to Christ before it is too late. This is the time! This is the hour! Let us humble ourselves before God's mighty presence and seek His face. Jesus Christ is at the door, and He is knocking. Will you answer Him with a surrendered and devoted heart?

SIGNS OF THE TIMES TESTIMONIES

REVIVAL IN MALAYSIA

The country of Malaysia is comprised of people from all over Asia. It is a mosaic of cultures, bringing together a vast array of beliefs and traditions. Sixty percent of the people are Muslim and 9 percent are Christian. According to Voice of the Martyrs, "Christianity is not illegal but it is illegal for Malays to convert to Christianity and for Christians to evangelize [Muslims]. Christian converts who are caught are confined to 'reeducation camps' that use brainwashing techniques, torture and propaganda to force them to return to Islam."[13]

Nevertheless, in the southeast of this nation, a great revival is taking place. This revival followed a spiritual activation, which King Jesus Ministry traveled to Malaysia to impart under the guidance of the Holy Spirit. Here is the testimony of one of the participants:

---

13. "Christians in Malaysia," Voice of the Martyrs, April 26, 2019, https://vom.com.au/christians-in-malaysia.

In the summer of 2017, at Petaling Jaya Stadium in Kuala Lumpur, the capital of Malaysia, we witnessed three days of incredible manifestations of God's kingdom, including salvations, deliverances, activations, and unusual miracles. This great revival actually began a short while beforehand, when we equipped two thousand pastors and leaders from all over the country in a supernatural encounter with Apostle Maldonado. In two days, he and his team helped us to build, restore, and affirm various areas of the church in Malaysia.

It all started with the restoration of the supernatural power of God. We expected to see the acceleration of His power, which helped break down old mentalities and mental strongholds that the church had carried for years. This allowed people to become spiritually activated. Leaders from all over the world came to see the manifestations of the kingdom. They anticipated seeing God's love and power pour over the people of Asia. These leaders knew that, through this great revival, they could heal the sick, cast out demons, and bring heaven into people's daily lives.

Many people gave testimonies at the encounter, but I remember one in particular from a missionary who lived in the mountains. Due to the unclean water of a nearby river, this woman had developed a condition in which her skin had become unnaturally dark. She participated in the event, and the next day, she began to feel a lot of heat and very sharp pains all over her body, and her skin returned to its natural color.

There was also a testimony from a woman who had heard Apostle Maldonado declare the power of the resurrection while watching Sid Roth's television program *It's Supernatural!* When she heard this declaration, she felt that she had to immediately apply it, so she declared it over a woman who was bedridden and near death from cancer. As soon as she made this declaration, life returned to the sick woman's body, and the Lord raised her up!

At that conference, the power of God manifested in the atmosphere so tangibly that there was a massive awakening. God's love restored, empowered, and brought a consuming fire to the whole nation. The fire of the Holy Spirit ignited a new passion for His presence and led the youth to cry out for more of the living God.

These two days of training prepared the atmosphere for what was about to happen at Petaling Jaya Stadium. Nearly sixty thousand people attended the supernatural gatherings over three days. Throughout the course of this event, there were ten thousand salvations. People responded to the Father's passionate call, running to the altar to surrender their hearts at the feet of Jesus—many for the first time, others returning to the Lord after having fallen away. Twenty thousand people were baptized in the Holy Spirit and forty thousand were activated in the supernatural. We documented five hundred and thirty testimonies of creative miracles and healings, including those of twenty-one people who stood up from their wheelchairs. Kuala Lumpur had a glimpse of God's will on earth as it is in heaven. Yes, we experienced revival in Malaysia, and we have seen the effects of this remarkable supernatural encounter on this great nation.

Since some of these new believers may face persecution, please join us in asking God to protect them and to continue the powerful work He has begun in Malaysia.

REVIVAL IN HONDURAS

Honduras is a violent country that needs the power of God and the love of Jesus to transform its culture. Voice of the Martyrs reported that eight pastors were murdered in that nation in the first half of 2013. Apparently, none of those murders was ever solved. At that time, the murder rate in Honduras was eighty-five out of every hundred thousand people.[14] A 2019 assessment by a human rights organization reported, "Violent crime is rampant in Honduras. Despite a downward trend in recent years, the murder rate remains among the highest in the world."[15]

Apostle Alejandro Espinoza of Honduras has been under the spiritual covering of King Jesus Ministry for fifteen years. The Holy Spirit gave me a word for them about a revival that would take place in their country. Stadiums would be filled and thousands of people would be saved. Today, that word is being fulfilled. They are seeing the greatest harvest of souls their nation has ever had.

Our ministry is based in San Pedro Sula, in northern Honduras. My wife and I were dentists for a number of years. As we practiced our profession, we realized that many of our patients had spiritual needs as well as physical ones. We told people who came to our clinic about God's power to save, heal, and deliver. In faith, they began to put a spiritual "demand," or claim, on His promises. Our clinic became like an altar as people were transformed by His supernatural power.

Then, God began to speak to me about becoming a pastor. That was the last thing I wanted, but God had other plans. I can now say that He has been real in our lives and very good to us. However, at the time, the most difficult part of going into ministry was leaving our clinic. We gave away everything related to our practice, including all the instruments, machines, and furniture. We were left with nothing, and we had to start from scratch. The transition was difficult, and we suffered sadness and rejection.

We traveled to King Jesus Ministry in Miami, longing for something new, fresh, and strong from God. When we arrived, He touched our lives and transformed our spirits. Thank God,

---

14. "Honduras: Pastors' Lives Threatened," Voice of the Martyrs, July 17, 2013, https://vom.com.au/honduras-pastors-lives-threatened/.
15. "Honduras: Events of 2018," *World Report 2019*, Human Rights Watch, https://www.hrw.org/world-report/2019/country-chapters/honduras.

we were able to overcome depression, loneliness, criticism, and much more. At King Jesus Ministry, we found fatherhood, purpose, destiny, and a calling to become part of the remnant that prepares the way for the coming of Jesus Christ.

In June 2005, we brought our church under the spiritual covering of Apostle Guillermo Maldonado and King Jesus Ministry, and we have seen an increase in our ministry since then. A distinct move of God began five years ago in which there was an acceleration of kingdom outreach and growth. In November 2016, we held a meeting in a gymnasium that seated five to six thousand people. In April 2017, we moved to an open area at Expocentro in San Pedro Sula, where fifteen thousand people gathered.

Then, at a Sunday meeting in June 2017, Apostle Maldonado imparted spiritual power to us and activated us anew to walk in the supernatural. He also gave us a prophetic word about a revival that was to occur in our nation. We received this word from God and believed it. This was a confirmation of the movement our ministry had been experiencing and an assurance that it would continue. In March 2018, we managed to fill the city's Estadio General Francisco Morazán, including the grassy area of the court, for an evangelistic event attended by more than twenty-five thousand people. We have moved from a religious mentality to a kingdom mentality and have broken cultural, mental, and financial barriers.

An abrupt but strong transition occurred with this acceleration. For the first time, we were holding events in public and free places. While the culture said we would need to charge a high admission fee in order to pay for the expenses required to hold the event at the stadium, God provided all we needed—more than fifty thousand dollars. We received donations from many people who got involved; some planted resources, while others provided their services.

In our ministry, we have seen the resurrection of the dead, with three documented cases. We have twenty-five ministries and several other national and international churches. We have multiplied ourselves through spiritual children, apostles, and prophets who have numerous churches. They, too, are expanding the kingdom throughout the territory. God has been faithful in every area of our life, and now we can see His glory shining through our ministry.

CHAPTER 3

THE TRUTH ABOUT JESUS'S COMING

How can we be assured that Jesus Christ will really return to earth? As I wrote in chapter 1, many preachers today deny the reality of the Lord's second coming. Therefore, I want to make certain your heart is founded on the truth. In this chapter, we will take a closer look at the biblical foundations of Jesus's return, the major end-time heresies, and the profound effects of accepting the truth about Christ's imminent coming.

I want to create an expectation of Jesus's return that will rouse you to prepare. We cannot say we believe in Christ but not in His second coming. And we cannot say we believe in His second coming while continuing to live in sin. Instead, as we respond to this crucial message, we must radically transform our lives. Allow the truths in this chapter to be like a mirror in which you see the real condition of your relationship with God so you can fully enter into His will and be ready for the coming of His Son.

THE REALITY OF JESUS'S FIRST COMING

As the Son of God, Jesus is both fully divine and fully human. He came to earth the first time when He was conceived by the Holy Spirit and born of a virgin. (See Isaiah 7:14; Luke 1:26–38.) He proclaimed the kingdom of God and died on a cross for our sins. Then, He rose again and ascended to heaven. These are historical facts that cannot be altered.

Many people of other religions acknowledge the existence of a "great teacher" named Jesus who lived in the first century, although they don't believe that He is God or that He rose again. Most Jews don't think their Messiah has yet come, not recognizing who Jesus actually is to them. Yet Christians believe these historical truths about Jesus Christ, and it has changed their lives forever. Part of the evidence that Jesus came the first time is the reality of the new birth within all who trust in Him as their Lord and Savior.

WITNESSES TO THE TRUTH ABOUT CHRIST'S COMING

We have noted that most of the prophesied end-time signs have already been fulfilled. Today, we are seeing the manifestation of the biblical prophecies and promises that remained to be completed. We are also receiving answers to many prayers—both prayers of the past and prayers of the present. Jesus is coming soon! This truth is not based on the opinions, traditions, or wisdom of man but on what God Himself has spoken and promised in His Word.

The Word of God is eternal, and it is a trustworthy source for understanding Christ's return.

For I testify to everyone who hears the words of the prophecy of this book: If anyone adds to these things, God will add to him the plagues that are written in this book; and if anyone takes away from the words of the book of this prophecy, God shall take away his part from the Book of Life, from the holy city, and from the things which are written in this book. (Revelation 22:18–19)

In addition to the Old Testament prophets who proclaimed the Messiah's second coming, the Scriptures provide us with several other powerful witnesses to the truth of Jesus's return. Again, this idea is not an empty theory or human calculation. It is found in the prophetic testimony of Jesus Himself; of His apostles, who heard it directly from Him; of God's angels; and of the Holy Spirit. Let us look at statements from each of these witnesses.

GOD'S WORD IS A TRUSTWORTHY SOURCE FOR UNDERSTANDING CHRIST'S SECOND COMING.

JESUS HIMSELF

Jesus announced His return in a number of places in the Gospels. (See, for example, Matthew 26:64; Mark 14:62; Luke 21:27.) He will not return as a servant to die for us again but as ruler over all. *"And He has on His robe and on His thigh a name written: KING OF KINGS AND LORD OF LORDS"* (Revelation 19:16). Let no one deceive you. Jesus confirmed He would return; He even expressed this fact in the book of Revelation when He said, *"I am the Alpha and the Omega, the Beginning and the End,…who is and who was and who is to come, the Almighty"* (Revelation 1:8).

JESUS'S APOSTLES

Jesus taught His disciples about His second coming. *"Now as He sat on the Mount of Olives, the disciples came to Him privately, saying, 'Tell us, when will these things be? And what will be the sign of Your coming, and of the end of the age?'"* (Matthew 24:3).

Later, the apostles, including Paul, instructed the church about the return of Christ. (See, for example, 1 Thessalonians 5:23; 2 Timothy

4:1–2; Hebrews 10:25; James 5:7–9; 1 Peter 1:13; 1 John 3:2; Jude 1:14.) In fact, they believed He would return in their day:

> *For this we say to you by the word of the Lord, that we who are alive and remain until the coming of the Lord will by no means precede those who are asleep. For the Lord Himself will descend from heaven with a shout, with the voice of an archangel, and with the trumpet of God. And the dead in Christ will rise first. Then we who are alive and remain shall be caught up together with them in the clouds to meet the Lord in the air. And thus we shall always be with the Lord.* (1 Thessalonians 4:15–17)

Note that those who have died in Christ will be taken up first, followed by those of us who are still alive. We will be transformed in an instant.

> *Behold, I tell you a mystery: We shall not all sleep, but we shall all be changed—in a moment, in the twinkling of an eye, at the last trumpet. For the trumpet will sound, and the dead will be raised incorruptible, and we shall be changed.* (1 Corinthians 15:51–52)

GOD'S ANGELS

> *Now when [Jesus] had spoken these things, while [the apostles] watched, He was taken up, and a cloud received Him out of their sight. And while they looked steadfastly toward heaven as He went up, behold, two men stood by them in white apparel, who also said, "Men of Galilee, why do you stand gazing up into heaven? This same Jesus, who was taken up from you into heaven, will so come in like manner as you saw Him go into heaven."* (Acts 1:9–11)

These "men" in white clothing were angels. They testified to the disciples that Jesus's departure confirmed His promise to come back. The manner of His leaving foreshadowed the manner of His return. Jesus left by ascending to the heavens, and He will return by way of the heavens.

Additionally, the angel who spoke to John when the apostle received the vision of Revelation affirmed the gospel message, which includes Jesus's second coming. John wrote, *"I fell at his feet to worship him. But he said to me, 'See that you do not do that! I am your fellow servant, and of your brethren who have the testimony of Jesus. Worship God! For the testimony of Jesus is the spirit of prophecy'"* (Revelation 19:10).

THE HOLY SPIRIT

"The Spirit and the bride say, 'Come!' And let him who hears say, 'Come!'" (Revelation 22:17). The Holy Spirit cries out in our hearts, testifying of Jesus's return. We who are the bride of Christ call on the Lord to come because the Spirit gives us the revelation of His impending appearance.

The voices of all these witnesses speak to us through the pages of the Bible. By the work of the Spirit, Scripture comes alive in our hearts. Through the testimony of Jesus Christ, His apostles, God's angels, and the Holy Spirit, the Word of God reveals to us that Christ's coming is near.

The Bible uses various phrases to describe Jesus's return and its accompanying events: *"the coming of the Lord"* and similar expressions (see, for example, Matthew 24:3; 1 Thessalonians 2:19; Hebrews 10:37; James 5:7–8; 2 Peter 1:16); *"caught up...to meet the Lord in the air"* (1 Thessalonians 4:17); *"the great and awesome day of the Lord"* (Acts 2:20); *"our Lord Jesus Christ's appearing"* (1 Timothy 6:14); and *"the revealing of the sons of God"* (Romans 8:19).

These biblical descriptions of Jesus's return actually encompass two different events. To understand the difference between these events, we need to review each of Jesus's three direct interventions on earth depicted in the Scriptures: first, Jesus's coming to His temple; second, Jesus's appearing; third, Jesus's second coming. All of these interventions are mentioned in the following passage:

"Behold, I send My messenger, and he will prepare the way before Me. And the Lord, whom you seek, will suddenly come to His

temple, even the Messenger of the covenant, in whom you delight.
Behold, He is coming," says the LORD *of hosts. "But who can endure*
the day of His coming? And who can stand when He appears? For
He is like a refiner's fire and like launderers soap."

(Malachi 3:1–2)

1. JESUS'S COMING TO HIS TEMPLE

Malachi's depiction of the Lord suddenly coming to His temple
refers to the Messiah's first arrival on earth as a human being more
than two thousand years ago. His birth is traditionally celebrated on
December 25, although, based on the biblical evidence, many scholars
think He may have been born in the fall, in September or October,
while others believe he was born during the summer.[16] I agree with
the first estimation because a fall date would coincide with the feast of
Tabernacles, which represents the fullness of time. *"When the fullness of*
the time had come, God sent forth His Son, born of a woman, born under
the law" (Galatians 4:4).

The generation of Israelites who lived at the time of Jesus's birth
already had prior knowledge of a coming Messiah, and there was a remnant of God's people that was prepared to receive Him. Yet Jesus's life
served as a turning point for all the people of earth, affecting the course
of human history in incalculable ways.

2. JESUS'S APPEARING

Jesus's second intervention on earth will be His appearance to take
the remnant of the church to heaven with Him before the great tribulation. There is a key distinction between Jesus's appearing and His
coming, so I want to make sure this point is clear:

---

16. See "When and Where Was Jesus Born?" Christianity.com, January 30, 2019, https://
www.christianity.com/jesus/birth-of-jesus/bethlehem/when-and-where-was-jesus-born.
html; Lesli White, "When Was Jesus Really Born?" Beliefnet, https://www.beliefnet.com/
faiths/christianity/articles/when-was-jesus-really-born.aspx; and "When Was Jesus Really
Born?" Jesus Film Project, December 21, 2017, https://www.jesusfilm.org/blog-and-stories/
when-jesus-really-born.html.

- Jesus's appearing is solely for His bride—those believers who are eagerly awaiting His return and are ready for Him.

- Jesus's coming is for the purpose of judging the world; thus, it is directed mainly at those who have remained on the earth during the tribulation.

The term most often used in Christian circles to describe the event in which Jesus will return for His bride is "the rapture." This expression is not found in the Bible but is derived from a Latin word, *rapio*, meaning "to seize or snatch in relation to an ecstasy of spirit or the actual removal from one place to another."[17] It has been used to describe what the coming of the Lord will be like for His church.

The Word of God presents two similes for Jesus's appearing that give us a sense of urgency regarding our need to be ready. The first simile is lightning: *"For as the lightning comes from the east and flashes to the west, so also will the coming of the Son of Man be"* (Matthew 24:27). This is vivid imagery because judgment is often quick, and lightning is an instantaneous phenomenon. Jesus will appear in the same way—suddenly and unexpectedly—to those who are not prepared and watching.

The other simile is that of a thief's stealthiness. *"For you yourselves know perfectly that the day of the Lord so comes as a thief in the night"* (1 Thessalonians 5:2). Someone who is sound asleep at night does not expect a thief to come to their house. Thieves often choose to rob homes under cover of darkness because they can more easily slip in and out, stealing valuables without anyone noticing until it's too late. Similarly, those who do not know Christ are spiritually asleep and living in darkness; therefore, they will be taken by surprise at His appearing. However, those who know Jesus and are living in His light will expect Him. Paul wrote, *"But you, brethren, are not in darkness, so that this Day should overtake you as a thief. You are all sons of light and sons of the day. We are not of the night nor of darkness. Therefore let us not sleep, as others*

---

17. "Where Did the Term 'Rapture' Come From?" Bible.org, January 1, 2001, https://bible.org/question/where-did-term-8216rapture'-come.

do, but let us watch and be sober" (1 Thessalonians 5:4–6). Likewise, Jesus urged us to *"watch and pray"* (Mark 13:33; see also Luke 21:36).

These illustrations of the quickness of lightning and the stealthiness of a thief send a clear message: be ready! *"Then two men will be in the field: one will be taken and the other left. Two women will be grinding at the mill: one will be taken and the other left. Watch therefore, for you do not know what hour your Lord is coming"* (Matthew 24:40–42).

Picture how the world will react when millions of believers suddenly disappear from the earth. Imagine the twenty-four-hour newscasts! There will be chaos all over the earth, with people desperately searching for their relatives, friends, and colleagues. A husband will wake up in the morning to find that his wife has disappeared. A pilot and copilot will be flying an airplane, and one will be taken while the other will remain. Students will be sitting in an auditorium at school when, suddenly, some of their classmates will vanish.

JESUS WILL APPEAR SUDDENLY AND UNEXPECTEDLY TO THOSE WHO ARE NOT PREPARED AND WATCHING.

As previously explained, after Jesus's appearing, the world will enter the great tribulation.

> *For then there will be great tribulation, such as has not been since the beginning of the world until this time, no, nor ever shall be.*
> (Matthew 24:21)

> *For when they say, "Peace and safety!" then sudden destruction comes upon them, as labor pains upon a pregnant woman. And they shall not escape.* (1 Thessalonians 5:3)

"Peace and safety" represent social and economic stability. There will be financial meltdowns on the earth, causing all currencies to lose their value. *"And I heard a voice in the midst of the four living creatures saying, 'A quart of wheat for a denarius* [about one day's wage for a worker], *and three quarts of barley for a denarius; and do not harm the oil and the wine'"* (Revelation 6:6). The world economy has already begun to experience shakiness. While national monetary policies or banks might provide some stability, we cannot put our trust in them for our provision, especially in these last days. We must trust only in the Lord to provide for us. He alone is our Rock. The world often thinks it has everything under control, but there will be social and economic devastation during the tribulation.

As for the believers who will remain on earth after the rapture because they were not ready for Jesus's appearing, they will know exactly what is happening because they will have read about it in God's Word or will have heard it preached. It will be horrible for them because they will have to make a fateful choice: either take the "mark of the beast,"[18] which would mean apostasy and condemnation to hell, or be killed for proclaiming the testimony of Jesus.

> *He causes all, both small and great, rich and poor, free and slave, to receive a mark on their right hand or on their foreheads, and that no one may buy or sell except one who has the mark or the name of the beast, or the number of his name.*　　　　(Revelation 13:16–17)

> *And I saw thrones, and they sat on them, and judgment was committed to them. Then I saw the souls of those who had been beheaded for their witness to Jesus and for the word of God, who had not worshiped the beast or his image, and had not received his mark on their*

---

18. This is the mark of the wicked world ruler called the Antichrist, who will be directed by Satan. "The antichrist is the 'man of lawlessness,' the 'son of destruction,' who will lead the world into rebellion against God (2 Thessalonians 2:3-10; Revelation 11:7) and deceive multitudes (Revelation 19:20)." See "Who Is the Antichrist and What Will His Rise Look Like?" Bible Study Tools, September 3, 2019, https://www.biblestudytools.com/bible-study/topical-studies/the-rise-of-the-antichrist.html.

foreheads or on their hands. And they lived and reigned with Christ
for a thousand years.   (Revelation 20:4)

Let me repeat: not all Christians are part of the bride of Christ. Only those who have been purified to become the remnant and who know how to discern the signs will be ready to be taken by Christ at His appearing. Jesus commanded His disciples, *"Watch therefore, and pray always that you may be counted worthy to escape all these things that will come to pass, and to stand before the Son of Man"* (Luke 21:36). These are times when we must be watching and praying for the signs of Jesus's appearing. Stay awake and alert, for He may appear at any time! Is your heart ready for the imminent return of the King?

3. JESUS'S SECOND COMING

When the seven years of tribulation have concluded, Jesus will come back to the earth once more. This time, He will return with the believers who were caught up to heaven with Him in the rapture. Jesus's coming will be seen clearly by all people throughout the world. His arrival will initiate the millennial period, during which He will rule the world.

Then the sign of the Son of Man will appear in heaven, and then all the tribes of the earth will mourn, and they will see the Son of Man coming on the clouds of heaven with power and great glory. And He will send His angels with a great sound of a trumpet, and they will gather together His elect from the four winds, from one end of heaven to the other.   (Matthew 24:30–31)

Behold, He is coming with clouds, and every eye will see Him, even they who pierced Him. And all the tribes of the earth will mourn because of Him. Even so, Amen.   (Revelation 1:7)

After the millennium will come the battle of Armageddon, in which Jesus will utterly defeat His enemies. That includes Satan, his demons, the Antichrist, and all other human beings who choose to join them in their rebellion. Jesus will cast Satan and his followers into the lake of fire. This will also be the time of final judgment for all people. (See Revelation 20:10–15.) Then, God will create new heavens and a new earth. The Lord will reign over a kingdom of peace, dwelling forever with His people. (See Revelation 21:1–3.)

To summarize, Jesus's first intervention on earth was His incarnation as a human being more than two thousand years ago, when He died on the cross, paid for our sins, rose again for our salvation, and ascended into heaven. His second intervention will be His appearing. This is when He will remove His bride, or the remnant of believers who have watched and prayed, turned from sin, and prepared the way for His return. His third intervention, after the great tribulation, will be His coming to rule the world in the millennium. After this, He will defeat Satan and administer the final judgment.

We have a decision to make. Will we meet Christ in the air at His appearing, or will we stay on earth during the tribulation and desperately long for His second coming?

HIS APPEARING IS FOR THE BRIDE.
HIS COMING IS TO JUDGE THE WORLD.

HERESIES OF THE END TIMES

As mentioned previously, Jesus's second coming will occur in the fullness of a God-ordained era that is approaching its apex. Everything is becoming aligned with the imminence of His return, which will usher in the millennium and set in motion the culmination of all things. "[Jesus] *made known to us the mystery of His* [God's] *will, according to His good pleasure which He purposed in Himself, that in the dispensation of the fullness of the times He might gather together in one all things in Christ, both which are in heaven and which are on earth—in Him"* (Ephesians 1:9–10). The devil hates this message. His greatest fear is knowing he will be completely defeated and sent to eternal punishment when the fullness of the times comes to a climax.

The enemy realizes he is running out of time! He is racing against the fullness of the times in order to delay his own destruction. Because he knows we are in the antechamber of Jesus's coming, he raises up arguments against the knowledge of God to prevent the remnant from gathering and fulfilling its purpose. He devises deceitful strategies to divert believers from keeping a pure faith.

Peter declared, *"Scoffers will come in the last days, walking according to their own lusts, and saying, 'Where is the promise of His coming? For since the fathers fell asleep, all things continue as they were from the beginning of creation'"* (2 Peter 3:3–4). Does this argument sound familiar to you? Do you know people who mock the idea of Jesus's coming or who say there is no basis for it?

The claim that Jesus will not return is a major heresy of the end times. A heresy is a perversion of truth that causes people to turn away from their faith in Christ. One version of this heresy is "kingdom is now" theology. According to adherents, Jesus already brought His kingdom to earth, so we are currently living in the millennial period, and Jesus does not need to return. This idea runs counter to the prophetic Scriptures, including Jesus's own statements about His coming.

Another dangerous end-time heresy is "super grace." This is the belief that "once saved, always saved." Under this view, there is no possibility of our falling away from Christ, even if we embrace a sinful lifestyle. In other words, no matter how we behave, we are assured of access to heaven and will be raptured at Jesus's appearing. This lie of the enemy causes some Christians to believe that because they supposedly cannot lose their salvation, there are no consequences for continuing to live in sin. As a result, they don't give the necessary attention to holy living and sanctification. *"But as He who called you is holy, you also be holy in all your conduct, because it is written, 'Be holy, for I am holy'"* (1 Peter 1:15–16).

It is obvious that Peter's prophecy about scoffers in the last days has been fulfilled. Those who deny Christ's coming and lead God's people astray have lost their sensitivity to the Holy Spirit, who constantly testifies to the nearness of the Lord's return. For someone to be deceived, they must first become desensitized to the things of God; they must come to a point where they stop believing His Word is true. Then, they begin to gratify the lusts of the flesh until they renounce the truth and depart altogether from their faith in Christ.

Make no mistake: false teachings and heresies about the end times can cause people to lose their faith in Christ and fall into sin. If you attend a church that denies the second coming, you should run from it because it is in error. Even if you don't realize it, you are being deceived! You must protect your position in Christ.

I could list many other false theologies, doctrines, and teachings that are leading multitudes to hell in these last days. No matter how the devil tries to dress up his deceit, the end purpose is the same: to make God look like a liar so human beings will turn away from Him. Will you believe the biblical witnesses, who affirm that Jesus is coming back? Or will you listen to the false voices of the world and the devil, who claim Jesus will not return?

Only an evil or fearful heart does not want Jesus to return. In order for a heart that once believed in Christ to become evil, it must have admitted deceit and sin into its life. Today, where do you stand spiritually? If you have been lax in your relationship with God, taking it for granted, repent immediately and begin to live according to His truth and righteousness.

If you have a spirit of fear regarding Christ's coming, that spirit is not from God. *"There is no fear in love; but perfect love casts out fear"* (1 John 4:18). Repent and ask God to deliver you from this spirit of fear and to establish His perfect love within you. *"To those who eagerly wait for Him He will appear a second time, apart from sin, for salvation"* (Hebrews 9:28).

PROFOUND EFFECTS OF BELIEVING THE TRUTH

When we believe God's Word and receive the truth about Christ's coming, it dramatically impacts our lives in the following ways:

IT AWAKENS EXPECTATION IN US

First, we will continually anticipate His appearing and act accordingly. If we truly believe that Jesus is coming back, we will be dedicated to seeking God, praying, worshipping, and evangelizing. Knowing that Jesus will return gives us a sense of immediacy that does not allow us to be spiritually asleep, but keeps us vigilant. Again, you cannot believe in the second coming and continue to live in sin. If you do, you have not yet received a revelation of the truth.

Many believers who are part of the remnant bride, and who live in areas of the world where there is much persecution against Christians, feel an urgency to preach the gospel. Among numerous other cases in Bhutan, a Buddhist country on the eastern edge of the Himalayas, two pastors were imprisoned in 2014 for preaching the gospel. Thankfully, they were later released.[19] In Indonesia, the home of two Christian brothers was attacked by approximately two hundred Muslims who were furious at them for helping bring more than a hundred Muslims in the area to Christ. The brothers were arrested and sentenced to three years in prison, where they were beaten by fellow inmates.[20]

There are countless similar stories of sacrifice for the sake of the gospel. What about you? Will you tell others of Christ's imminent return and the salvation He offers them?

IT GENERATES A HOPE THAT PURIFIES AND PREPARES US

We know that when He is revealed, we shall be like Him, for we shall see Him as He is. And everyone who has this hope in Him purifies himself, just as He is pure. (1 John 3:2–3)

---

19. "Bhutan: Pastor Imprisoned for Evangelism Released," Voice of the Martyrs, February 19, 2015, https://vom.com.au/bhutan-pastor-imprisoned-for-evangelism-released.
20. "Indonesia: Update – Two Indonesian Christians Sentenced to Three Years Behind Bars for Evangelism," October 9, 2013, Voice of the Martyrs, https://vom.com.au/indonesia-update-two-indonesian-christians-sentenced-to-three-years-behind-bars-for-evangelism.

Many nations, including America, are in great need of purification and renewal. A report from Barna Group stated that Americans are living in an increasingly "pornified" popular culture. One result is that young people have a casual attitude toward watching or talking about pornography.[21] If there is a generation that needs to purify its heart, it is the present one.

Additionally, in our culture, sinful behaviors have been legalized. This state of affairs has led to widespread iniquity and injustice. The devil is attempting to make hell itself legal on earth. We must not allow ourselves to be caught up in his deceptions. If you hold the conviction that the Lord will return and you desire to be part of the remnant that is ready to receive Him, you will allow the Holy Spirit to continually purify your heart and mind, cleansing you of all defilement and impurity.

For the grace of God that brings salvation has appeared to all men, teaching us that, denying ungodliness and worldly lusts, we should live soberly, righteously, and godly in the present age, looking for the blessed hope and glorious appearing of our great God and Savior Jesus Christ. (Titus 2:11–13)

IT REKINDLES THE FIRE OF OUR FIRST LOVE

As mentioned previously, many Christians in countries that are hostile to the gospel share their faith with a sense of urgency and great courage. However, many Christians in countries that are friendlier to the gospel have become spiritually cool. Let's look again at the current generation of young people in America. According to a Barna study conducted over a span of ten years, of those aged eighteen to twenty-nine with a Christian background, 22 percent are "prodigals," or ex-Christians; 30 percent are "nomads," or lapsed Christians; 38 percent are "habitual church-goers," but without foundational core beliefs

---

21. "Teens & Young Adults Use Porn More Than Anyone Else," Barna Group, January 28, 2016, www.barna.com/research/teens-young-adults-use-porn-more-than-anyone-else.

or corresponding behavior; and only 10 percent are "resilient disciples" who are committed to Jesus.[22]

Believers in all age groups are in urgent need of returning to Jesus as their *"first love"* (Revelation 2:4), with hearts ignited by the Holy Spirit's fire. When the Lord rekindles our hearts, we return to the same devotion and passion for Jesus we had when we were first saved. This necessary vital devotion will come from a revelation of the truth concerning Christ's imminent coming. A high percentage of Christians are spiritually asleep and must be awakened to join the remnant that prepares the way of the Lord!

IT BRINGS THE FEAR OF GOD

"The fear of the LORD *is to hate evil; pride and arrogance and the evil way and the perverse mouth I hate"* (Proverbs 8:13). In much of the church, a genuine fear of God—a deep sense of awe and reverence toward Him—has been lost. Consequentially, many believers' resistance against temptation and evil has dissolved. A number of Christians now consider sin to be acceptable, so that they tolerate the wrongdoing they once hated. When we start calling *"evil good, and good evil"* (Isaiah 5:20), we ultimately become insensitive to sin. We look for excuses to gratify our fleshly desires, and we fail to see the dangerous consequences of compromising the truth. Remember, there are people who are living a sinful lifestyle who still believe that Jesus will take them to heaven in the rapture. This is a deception! A knowledge of the truth regarding Jesus's return will restore the fear of God in people's hearts and lead them to reject sin, to repent, and to be restored in their relationships with the Lord. Then, they will call evil what it truly is: evil. And their lives will manifest the righteousness, peace, and joy of God's kingdom.

---

22. "Only 10% of Christian Twentysomethings Have Resilient Faith," Barna Group, September 24, 2019, https://www.barna.com/research/of-the-four-exile-groups-only-10-are-resilient-disciples.

IT PROTECTS OUR HEARTS FOR HIS APPEARING

When our hearts are established in God's truth through the revelation of Jesus's coming, we will not be taken in by false theologies and end-time heresies. *"Now may the God of peace Himself sanctify you completely; and may your whole spirit, soul, and body be preserved blameless at the coming of our Lord Jesus Christ"* (1 Thessalonians 5:23).

Do you believe in Christ's return? Are you ready for this unprecedented, impending event? People who believe in His return are not casual about their faith. They are on fire for God! They want to serve Him wholeheartedly. They want to worship Him with their fellow believers. If everyone believed Jesus was returning soon, there would not be a single empty seat in the churches, and all the prayer services would be full. Every Christian must be committed to Jesus, and the whole church needs to evangelize as if there were no tomorrow. We must be busy with God's business. This is the time to say yes to God. This is the time to consecrate yourself to Christ. Let us tell everyone that Jesus is coming back soon!

Maranatha! Come, Lord Jesus!

SUMMARY

+ Most of the prophesied end-time signs have already been fulfilled. Today, we are seeing the manifestation of the biblical
  prophecies and promises that remained to be completed, and
  we are receiving many answers to prayer.

+ In addition to the Old Testament prophets who proclaimed the
  Messiah's second coming, the Scriptures provide us with these
  powerful witnesses to the truth of Jesus's return: Jesus Himself,
  Jesus's apostles, God's angels, and the Holy Spirit.

+ Jesus's three direct interventions on earth are the following:
  (1) His coming to His temple; (2) His appearing; (3) His second
  coming.

+ Jesus's appearing refers to His removal of the remnant, the bride
  of Christ, from the earth. Jesus's coming refers to His return to
  earth after the great tribulation to initiate the millennium and
  judge the world.

+ A heresy is a perversion of truth that causes people to turn away
  from their faith in Christ.

+ Two end-time heresies are the theology of "kingdom now,"
  which claims we are currently in the millennium and denies the
  return of the Lord, and the theology of "super grace," which says
  that once we are saved, we are always saved, even if we embrace
  a sinful lifestyle.

+ Many sins have been legalized in our day; this state of affairs has
  led to widespread iniquity and injustice.

+ When we acknowledge the truth about Christ's coming, it produces the following effects: it awakens expectation in us; it gen-
  erates a hope that purifies and prepares us; it rekindles the fire
  of our first love for Christ; it brings the fear of God; and it pro-
  tects our hearts for Jesus's appearing.

SIGNS OF THE TIMES TESTIMONIES

In the midst of a world that "calls evil good, and good evil," young people are becoming confused about many things, including their sexuality, and they are losing their God-given identity. Unfortunately, they often lack the loving guidance of a parent who can affirm their true identity. Yet God's purifying fire has the power to reveal the truth to their hearts and transform them completely, enabling them to become witnesses to others who are trapped in the enemy's deceit.

The men in the following testimonies both fell prey to a spirit of homosexuality, but their lives were restored through the ministry of Apostle Ángel Beriau from Paraguay, who is under the spiritual covering of King Jesus Ministry. The first testimony is from Hugo Ayala.

At age forty-nine, I can say that God has given me a new life. For twenty-five years, I was in hell, immersed in a world of homosexuality, alcohol, and drugs. I was hospitalized twice for suicide attempts, twice for alcoholism, and once for a cocaine overdose.

My problems started when I was very young. At five years of age, I was already spying on my father while he was bathing or in his room. In elementary school, I was part of a group of friends who engaged in a lot of groping. At the age of nine, I was even involved in penetration activities. As a teenager, I masturbated up to eight times a day. When I was twenty-one, I started going to bars, discos, and private meetings for gays. At twenty-four, I had my first partner, a thirty-three-year-old man who took me away from the bar environment for seven years. However, when that relationship ended, I returned to the gay scene and to using cocaine.

I had four close friends, and we were inseparable. From Friday to Sunday, we would go to private parties, where there were orgies and unlimited drugs and alcohol. As a result of this unbridled life, two of these friends died of AIDS, and the other two overdosed. I was the only survivor of our group.

One Sunday, I arrived home at noon, heavily drugged after a four-day party. The man I'd been with had stolen all my money, as well as my supply of cocaine. My body was asking for more drugs, but I couldn't go out and buy any because I had no funds. I hit bottom. All I could hear in my thoughts was, "Kill yourself, kill yourself, kill yourself." I couldn't take it anymore, so I decided to end my life. However, as I was trying to throw myself from the second floor of my house, I heard another voice tell me repeatedly, "Son, I love you; don't do it," until I gave up.

I opened my bedroom window, and my neighbor from across the street, whom I had never seen before, came into view. The same voice I'd heard telling me not to kill myself insisted, "Cross the street and go to My servant." When I went there, my neighbor, Apostle Ángel Beriau, welcomed me with great love, the love of Christ. He hugged me tightly and began to pray for me.

We went back to my house, grabbed a bag, filled it with all my pornography, sex toys, and alcohol, and threw it away. Apostle Beriau then took me to his church, where they were having an encounter with God during a retreat. There, I heard people give testimonies of their deliverance, and this gave me hope. I began to go through a process of healing and deliverance with Apostle Beriau and a powerful intercessory team at his church. However, I had a relapse, and the apostle told me that I had to decide between Christ and the world. He suggested that I change my phone number in order to break the cord that was tying me to my past.

That day, I decided for Christ. Eight years have passed, and I have never gone back. In 2013, I heard a teaching about making faith declarations, and this led me to declare that, within a year, I would be engaged to be married to a woman. (When I was living a destructive lifestyle, I had never been attracted to women.) Yet, not even a year went by before I had a girlfriend. In 2014, I declared that I would marry her and become a father, and everything has happened just as I professed. My life is a demonstration of the transforming power of God.

Apostle Beriau adds, "This testimony is very important in our church because Hugo's wife is my daughter Juliet. Today, Hugo is an elder and my daughter is a pastor, and they bear much fruit for the Lord. We really believe in the power of God to transform people."

Another member of this church, Eduardo Cabral, had a similar experience after being abused by a cousin. He lived a lifestyle of homosexuality, alcohol, and drugs until he had a radical encounter with God. Now he is happily married and faithfully following the Lord.

I was born into a loving home, and my early childhood was very peaceful. However, I soon had an experience that marked my life so severely it followed me into adulthood. When I was just four years old, one of my cousins, who was seventeen, taught me a "secret game" that was nothing but child sexual abuse. He told me that if I liked it, I should not tell anyone. My mother noticed irritations in my genital area and took me to the doctor, but they couldn't find the cause. She asked me what was wrong, but I kept it a secret.

Soon afterward, my cousin disappeared, but I continued to play the "game" with other children; however, now, I was the one who taught it, with the key phrase, "If you like it, don't tell anyone." From older children, I learned about oral sex and penetration. Homosexuality was instilled in my mind and emotions. Also, at the age of eleven, in my father's office, I discovered a lot of pornographic material, which influenced me.

When I was twelve, I met a girl who became my girlfriend. However, when I was sixteen, I traveled to the United States, leaving her behind. There, I saw transvestites and men holding hands. I noticed effeminate men on the beach with their partners—and I learned they lived in mansions. All of this behavior seemed to be considered normal.

After returning to my country, I began studies at a university. There, I formed a group of "elite" friends, composed of children of ambassadors, presidents, noted politicians, businessmen, and farmers, with whom I began to smoke and drink. In front of everyone else, I acted like a "man," but, secretly, I was a homosexual. I would choose my prey, and the more masculine, attractive, and difficult to win over they were, the more exciting!

I graduated with a degree in ecological engineering, and I was hired as the national business director of a renowned international economic organization. I was sent to a distant city, where I met a gay billionaire footballer. This was the most debauched and alcohol-ridden period of my life. My unrestrained lifestyle led me to bankruptcy, and I had to start all over again. I returned to my home city, where I met a man and fell in love. We got married in a country where homosexual unions are legal, but the marriage did not last. I kept organizing private parties in order to have as much sex as possible, while using drugs heavily. My parents hardly ever visited me because it was too difficult for them to see me in this destructive state. However, my mother prayed for me for seventeen years.

One day, I used so much cocaine that my nose started bleeding nonstop. I couldn't breathe and was foaming at the mouth. I almost died! Alone in my house, I knelt and asked God for help. A week later, I got a call from an architect who was working on a building site at the church where she served as an elder. She asked me to do an environmental impact study. After my evaluation, I told her, "Your institution does not comply with environmental requirements. You could be sanctioned." However, something inside me told me to help them.

At that time, I smoked close to forty cigarettes a day. However, from the moment I arrived at the church, every time I tried to smoke, I would become nauseous. I soon stopped partying. While I was working for the church, a congress of pastors and other leaders from all over the country and other nations was held, and the architect invited me to evaluate the environmental impact of this massive event. There, the Holy Spirit touched my heart, and I saw impressive miracles. While we were still at this congress, the architect asked me to go to one more meeting at the church. I didn't really desire to attend, but I agreed because I wanted to finish the job, get paid, and never go back to that church. After I arrived at the meeting, it took only one word for me to yield to God. Apostle Beriau said, "God loves you more than you know." I felt something inside me break. My chest seemed to open up and I could breathe. A type of oppression left me, and I broke down in tears.

In his sermon, the apostle talked about Genesis and creation, and I received the revelation that God had created me to be a man. I felt tremendous joy in realizing that the homosexual life was a lie. I received that word of freedom, was baptized, and left the "old man" in the waters. God's power took away my vices and cleansed me of all mental impurity. I emerged with the identity of a child of God. I did go through a difficult process of healing and spiritual transformation, but I never ceased to fight the enemy's tricks.

I decided that by 2019, I would be married to a woman, and one day, I met a wonderful lady. Today, we are happily married, building our union on the purposes of the Father and committed to serve and worship Him. My house, which had been a place of destruction, was transformed into a House of Peace,[23] where the love of the Father reigns, where the Holy Spirit dwells, and where Jesus Christ has total authority.

23. A House of Peace refers to the home of a member of King Jesus International Ministry or its associate churches who welcomes neighbors, relatives, and friends for the purpose of sharing the gospel of the kingdom—teaching the Word of God and imparting His power. The same anointing, supernatural power, and presence of God that are found in the main King Jesus Ministry church manifest there.

CHAPTER 4

THE SIGN OF HIS COMING

Then Jesus went out and departed from the temple,
and His disciples came up to show Him the buildings of the temple.
And Jesus said to them, "Do you not see all these things?
Assuredly, I say to you, not one stone shall be left here upon
another, that shall not be thrown down."
—Matthew 24:1–2

Based on this prophetic declaration, Jesus's disciples believed that His second coming would coincide with the destruction of the temple in Jerusalem. As Jews, the temple was so sacred to them that they thought, "When the temple is destroyed, the end of the world will come."

Shortly after hearing this prophecy, the disciples asked Jesus three questions about the end times:

Now as He sat on the Mount of Olives, the disciples came to Him
privately, saying, "Tell us, when will these things be? And what will
be the sign of Your coming, and of the end of the age?"

(Matthew 24:3)

Before we discuss Jesus's answers to these vital questions, we need to define what a sign is.

WHAT IS A SIGN?

A sign is not an end in itself but rather points to something or someone. It might function as a portent, which refers to "something that foreshadows a coming event" or "a prophetic indication or significance." In the context of this book, the following definition of a sign is also very appropriate: "something material or external that stands for or signifies something spiritual." A biblical sign always points to a higher reality. Every sign that comes from God points back to Him. Over the millennia, He has given various signs to His people so they can be aware of how He is moving and what is coming in the future. Ultimately, all the signs that Jesus revealed point to His appearing, His coming, and the end of the age.

Biblical signs can help us understand why certain events are happening in the world. However, signs are not always easy for us to discern because, in many cases, we need the revelation of the Holy Spirit to comprehend them. As I mentioned previously, to this end, God has given the church the ministries of the apostle and the prophet. One of their roles is to explain the signs of the times.

> **THE SPIRITUAL SIGNS WE ARE SEEING TODAY POINT TO JESUS'S APPEARING AND, ULTIMATELY, TO HIS SECOND COMING AND THE END OF THE AGE.**

Again, natural man cannot understand these signs because the origin of the signs is supernatural. This is why most world leaders today are perplexed about the economic, environmental, and health crises affecting the world, and why they have no sustainable answers for them. They don't recognize the spiritual elements involved.

With the state of the world in these last days, we cannot be casual or apathetic about our faith. We cannot neglect to fast and pray for God's direction and for His will to be done on earth as it is in heaven. If you believe in Jesus's appearing, then you must be looking for the signs that announce it. Jesus was clear that we should watch and pray when that time is near.

WARNING SIGNS

The closer we draw to the coming of the Lord, the more frequent and intense the signs will become. It is imperative that we not only are aware of these signs, but also know their significance. If we do not have a prophetic understanding of God's signs, we will lack the perspective of the end times that is necessary for conducting our lives in these crucial times.

I believe that one end-time sign is the extreme weather our world has been experiencing. The United States Environmental Protection Agency states, "Rising global average temperature is associated with widespread changes in weather patterns. Scientific studies indicate that extreme weather events such as heat waves and large storms are likely to become more frequent or more intense with human-induced climate change."[24] Climate change has caused the oceans to warm up, contributing to an increase in the number of intense hurricanes, including category 4 and 5 storms. This trend will continue.[25]

Although the frequency and strength of earthquakes has apparently not changed, people are now more aware of them because we have better

---

24. "Climate Change Indicators," Environmental Protection Agency, August 2, 2016, https://www.epa.gov/climate-indicators/weather-climate.
25. Doyle Rice, "Are Category 5 Hurricanes Such as Dorian the 'New Normal'?" *USA Today*, September 11, 2019, https://www.usatoday.com/story/news/nation/2019/09/11/category-5-hurricanes-storms-like-dorian-new-normal/2275423001/.

technology and communication.[26] Between 2000 and 2019, there have been twenty-four earthquakes measuring 8 or higher on the Richter scale,[27] causing much destruction. Events like these that show mankind its vulnerability and need for God should cause us to repent and seek Him. Shortly after Jesus spoke to the crowds about discerning the times, He stated, *"Or those eighteen on whom the tower in Siloam fell and killed them, do you think that they were worse sinners than all other men who dwelt in Jerusalem? I tell you, no; but unless you repent you will all likewise perish"* (Luke 13:4–5).

Natural disasters are beyond our ability to control, and climate change is causing many worrying changes to the earth's environment. It is inevitable that we will endure more weather-related catastrophes. God is speaking to us through these conditions, showing us our human frailty and need for Him as our Creator and Sustainer.

The remnant that God is gathering must be able to discern the purpose of end-time signs and prepare for the Lord's appearing. While we may experience some of the effects of these warning signs, we are not appointed for judgment or the tribulation. We are appointed for rapture!

THIS IS THE HOUR WHEN WE ESPECIALLY NEED GOD'S SUPERNATURAL POWER.

THREE QUESTIONS ABOUT JESUS'S COMING

Let's now return to the passage in Matthew 24 that we looked at previously and explore the three specific questions Jesus's disciples asked Him regarding the signs of His return:

26. "Is Earthquake Activity Increasing?" British Geological Survey, http://www.earthquakes.bgs.ac.uk/news/EQ_increase.html.
27. "New Earthquake Hazards Program," United States Geological Survey (USGS), https://www.usgs.gov/natural-hazards/earthquake-hazards/lists-maps-and-statistics.

Then Jesus went out and departed from the temple, and His disciples came up to show Him the buildings of the temple. And Jesus said to them, "Do you not see all these things? Assuredly, I say to you, not one stone shall be left here upon another, that shall not be thrown down." Now as He sat on the Mount of Olives, the disciples came to Him privately, saying, "Tell us, when will these things be? And what will be the sign of Your coming, and of the end of the age?" (Matthew 24:1–3)

"WHEN WILL THESE THINGS BE"?

The first question was, *"Tell us, when will these things be?"* (Matthew 24:3). Jesus explained that events would unfold over time. Some of the signs He mentioned in Matthew 24 have already taken place. For instance, the prophecy about the destruction of the temple was fulfilled exactly as Jesus had predicted when the Roman general Titus besieged Jerusalem in AD 70. As noted earlier, some prophecies having to do with the persecution of the church (see verse 9) were fulfilled in the first century or during the Middle Ages, and others are being fulfilled today in countries where Christianity is outlawed or Christians are ostracized.

In chapter 5 of this book, we will review additional end-time signs. However, let us keep in mind that many prophecies concerning Christ's coming have been fulfilled in the past century. Again, one of the greatest events signaling the end times was the restoration of the nation of Israel in 1948, which occurred due to God's supernatural intervention.

I want to make clear here that, although God has a special plan for Israel, the Jewish people will be saved only through Jesus's sacrifice on the cross, the same requirement that applies to everyone. They need to repent, accept Jesus as their Messiah, and be filled with the Holy Spirit because the only way to the heavenly Father is through Jesus. (See John 14:6.) However, the fact that the nation of Israel has been restored means that the clock is ticking because end-time prophecies would not be complete without this promised restoration. End-time signs continue to be fulfilled in our day. It is happening before our eyes.

"WHAT WILL BE THE SIGN OF YOUR COMING, AND OF THE END OF THE AGE?"

The second and third questions can be addressed together because their answers are much more integrated. The disciples even merged these questions into one inquiry: *"And what will be the sign of Your coming* [Jesus's appearing], *and of the end of the age* [Jesus's second coming]?" (Matthew 24:3). There is a clear distinction between the sign of Jesus's appearing and the sign of His second coming because they point to separate events. Remember, Jesus's appearing is for gathering His remnant bride, and His coming is for judging and ruling the world.

THE SIGN OF JESUS'S APPEARING: DIVINE "SHAKINGS"

Prior to Jesus's appearing, divine "shakings" are to come upon the earth and its people. These shakings will occur in three stages. In chapter 3, we talked about one aspect of the tremors, the shaking of the global economy. During these shakings, whatever can be loosed—whatever does not have a strong foundation in Christ—will sway and fall. We have already gone through the preliminary stage of shaking and are currently experiencing the intermediate stage. We are slowly moving toward the commencement of the final shaking:

For thus says the LORD of hosts: "Once more (it is a little while) I will shake heaven and earth, the sea and dry land; and I will shake all nations, and they shall come to the Desire of All Nations, and I will fill this temple with glory," says the LORD of hosts. (Haggai 2:6–7)

These verses describe a shaking that will occur in every dimension and sphere of life. Wherever there is life, there will be trembling!

God will shake the heavens, the earth, the seas, and the weather. Heavenly bodies will fall. The earth will shift due to earthquakes, so that no mountain or island will be left in its place. The boundaries of the oceans will be altered.

God will shake nations, governments, institutions, the world economy, families, and individuals, including people's relationships and health.

God will shake the devil and his demons. After the shaking we are currently experiencing, evil spirits will walk on the earth because they will have fallen from the second heaven. (See, for example, Isaiah 14:12–14; Luke 10:18; Revelation 8:10; 9:1.) Again, everything that is not established in Christ will be shaken loose and fall. He is the only firm rock!

> But why do you call Me "Lord, Lord," and not do the things which I say? Whoever comes to Me, and hears My sayings and does them, I will show you whom he is like: He is like a man building a house, who dug deep and laid the foundation on the rock. And when the flood arose, the stream beat vehemently against that house, and could not shake it, for it was founded on the rock. But he who heard and did nothing is like a man who built a house on the earth without a foundation, against which the stream beat vehemently; and immediately it fell. And the ruin of that house was great. (Luke 6:46–49)

END-TIME SHAKINGS ARE RELATED TO THREE THINGS: THE SIGNS OF THE TIMES, JUDGMENT, AND THE GLORY OF GOD.

God is using the shaking we are now experiencing to refine believers so that they will be purified to become the remnant that is ready for Jesus's appearing. However, the main purpose of the shaking is to judge the people of the world for their sin and rebellion against Him. If you have been going through a shaking in your personal life, family, finances, or health, then rejoice! God is purifying you as the remnant bride. Keep your lamp burning!

Jesus confirmed Haggai's prophecy about the shaking that would occur on the earth when He said, *"Immediately after the tribulation of those days the sun will be darkened, and the moon will not give its light; the stars will fall from heaven, and the powers of the heavens will be shaken"* (Matthew 24:29). The sun, the moon, and the stars are the three elements that give light to the earth; moreover, the sun and moon are the celestial bodies that we use to mark the seasons, days, and hours. As such, they represent mankind's understanding and comprehension, which will also be shaken. Everything will be darkened! Again, people will not understand what is happening in the world unless they look to God and receive His revelation. They will be disoriented and unfocused, not knowing where to turn.

In contrast, God's remnant will not become bewildered, even by the absence of light from the sun, moon, and stars, because they will have the light of Christ within them to direct their steps in those devastating times. They will light their lamps of vigil, prayer, and the Word in preparation for His appearing. That is the character of the remnant Jesus will take away to heaven with Him! We do not know how long the final period of shaking will last before the rapture occurs, but we do know that at its conclusion, in the fullness of this era, Jesus will appear for His purified bride.

THE SIGN OF JESUS'S COMING: THE PREACHING OF THE GOSPEL TO THE WHOLE WORLD

While the sign of Jesus's appearing is the shaking of all things, the sign of His coming, and ultimately of the end of the age, is the preaching of the gospel throughout the world: *"And this gospel of the kingdom will be preached in all the world as a witness to all the nations, and then the end will come"* (Matthew 24:14).

How will the preaching of the gospel to the whole world be accomplished? We read in the book of Daniel, *"But you, Daniel, shut up the words, and seal the book until the time of the end; many shall run to and fro, and knowledge shall increase"* (Daniel 12:4). God told Daniel to seal the prophecy *"until the time of the end."* I believe that when Israel became a nation, that seal was broken. Following this was the fulfillment of the prophecy about increased knowledge in the world, which has led to an explosion in the development of technology.

Thanks to technology, what we previously couldn't have accomplished in decades or even centuries to spread the gospel, we can now accomplish in a year, a month, or a week. Much of the world today has access to the Internet. Even in countries that don't yet have a high percentage of coverage, like China and India, efforts are being made to provide the capability. For example, India has 1.3 billion people, but only 450 million currently have access to the Internet. "With only 36 per cent internet penetration, there is still much headroom for growth," says a report by the Internet and Mobile Association of India.[28] Such expanded access would give millions more the potential to hear the gospel. Increasingly, electronic technology is designed to operate in real time, or in the now, so that it is not only more global but also more instantaneous.

> **WHILE THE SIGN OF JESUS'S APPEARING IS THE SHAKING OF ALL THINGS, THE SIGN OF HIS COMING AND OF THE END OF THE AGE IS THE PREACHING OF THE GOSPEL THROUGHOUT THE WORLD.**

We now have the potential to reach billions of people with the good news of the kingdom! The Great Commission of bringing the gospel to all nations (see Matthew 28:19) is being accomplished.

---

28. Megha Mandavia, "India Has Second Highest Number of Internet Users After China: Report," *The Economic Times*, September 26, 2019, https://economictimes.indiatimes.com/tech/internet/india-has-second-highest-number-of-internet-users-after-china-report/articleshow/71311705.cms?utm_source=contentofinterest&utm_medium.

The statistics about the growth of Christianity are not particularly rousing in countries like the United States. However, in places like the Islamic Republic of Iran and The People's Republic of China, it is a totally different picture. Even though the governments of these nations are restricting Christians' use of technology or using technology to monitor the movements of their citizens, God is working, and the church continues to grow.[29] Iran is ranked among the top-ten countries that persecute Christians,[30] but the church there is one of the fastest-growing in the world.[31] China has stepped up intense persecution of Christians.[32] Still, the number of believers in that nation may be as high as one hundred and fifty million.[33]

Even in Europe, where Christianity has been in decline for decades, church attendance is reportedly "skyrocketing" in certain areas due to the conversion of Iranian and Afghan immigrants, whose religious background is Islam.[34]

The fact that people throughout the world will hear the gospel message through advanced technology or other methods before Christ comes back does not mean that everyone will be saved. However, it does mean that everyone will have an opportunity to hear the gospel at

29. See, for example, "Iran: More Restrictions, More Growth," Voice of the Martyrs, February 25, 2020, https://vom.com.au/iran-more-restrictions-more-growth; "China: Shandong Authorities Ban Online Preaching," Voice of the Martyrs, March 12, 2020, https://vom.com.au/china-shandong-authorities-ban-online-preaching/; "Christianity Grows in China Despite Persecution," Persecution.org, International Christian Concern, April 29 2019, https://www.persecution.org/2019/04/29/christianity-grows-china-despite-persecution/.
30. "World Watch List," Open Doors, https://www.opendoorsusa.org/christian-persecution/world-watch-list/.
31. "Iran: Government Concerned with the Growth of Christianity," Voice of the Martyrs, July 25, 2019, https://vom.com.au/iran-government-concerned-with-the-growth-of-christianity/.
32. "China: Weifang Honours Areas for Cracking Down on Religion," Voice of the Martyrs, January 23, 2020, https://vom.com.au/china-weifang-honours-areas-for-cracking-down-on-religion/.
33. Eugene Bach and Brother Zhu, *The Underground Church* (New Kensington, PA: Whitaker House, 2014), 31.
34. "Europe: Muslim Conversions Spike Church Growth," Voice of the Martyrs, March 15, 2017, https://vom.com.au/europe-muslim-conversions-spike-church-growth/.

least once. No one will have an excuse on judgment day that they never heard the message.

Note that the Bible says the end will come when the *"gospel of the kingdom* [has been] *preached in all the world"* (Matthew 24:14). Unfortunately, the gospel of the kingdom is not the gospel that is being preached in many places today. Instead, people are hearing substitute gospels. Among these are the self-help gospel, the motivational gospel, the historical gospel (a belief in the historical facts of Jesus's first-century life, without an acknowledgment of the presence of the resurrected Christ and the Holy Spirit in believers' lives today), and the poverty gospel, as well as the gospel of words without manifestations (a lack of accompanying miracles) and the gospel of "super grace," which was mentioned in the previous chapter as one of the end-time heresies. These are powerless gospels!

THE END OF THE WORLD CANNOT COME UNLESS EVERY PERSON ON EARTH HAS HEARD THE GOSPEL OF THE KINGDOM.

"For I am not ashamed of the gospel of Christ, for it is the power of God to salvation for everyone who believes, for the Jew first and also for the Greek" (Romans 1:16). The gospel of the kingdom is not one that simply makes us "feel good." Moreover, it does not consist of mere *"persuasive words of human wisdom, but in demonstration of the Spirit and of power"* (1 Corinthians 2:4). It comes with supernatural evidence, such as miracles, signs, and wonders.

God has entrusted to every single believer the task of preaching this gospel of the kingdom. He did not give this assignment to only a select few. Neither did He choose world leaders or governments to get the job done. He chose each member of His church to accomplish this mighty work through the power of His Spirit.

> And Jesus came and spoke to [the disciples], *saying, "All authority has been given to Me in heaven and on earth. Go therefore and make disciples of all the nations, baptizing them in the name of the Father and of the Son and of the Holy Spirit, teaching them to observe all things that I have commanded you; and lo, I am with you always, even to the end of the age."*
>
> (Matthew 28:18–20; see also Mark 16:15)

The world is in crisis. People are waiting for us, God's children, to tell them about Christ. (See Romans 10:14–15.) The gospel of the kingdom is simple, practical, and powerful, and the supreme task of the church is to bring it to the whole world. The truth of the gospel is confirmed by the resurrection of Jesus! We need to go and demonstrate the power of His resurrection. This is what it means to say, "Come, Lord Jesus" with the Spirit, as the purified bride of Christ!

PREACHING THE GOSPEL EFFECTIVELY IN THE END TIMES

Some of the ways in which Christians are trying to preach the gospel today are deeply ineffective. The errors usually come from attempting to spread the good news of the kingdom according to human strength and judgment rather than by the direction and power of the Holy Spirit. Let us look at some foundational elements of preaching the gospel effectively in these end times.

BE PART OF GOD'S END-TIME REVIVAL

For the church to preach the gospel throughout the world before the return of Christ, it must experience true revival and be part of the great outpouring of God's Spirit. Revival can be defined as "an act or instance of reviving" or "the state of being revived, such as a new presentation or publication of something old." For the church, revival means a return to its original purpose, only in a larger dimension. This is because revival is always accompanied by a new work of God. If what we experience in the church has previously happened in the same way, then no matter how wonderful it may be, it cannot be considered revival.

The Bible tells us that "[Jesus] *has made us kings and priests to His God and Father*" (Revelation 1:6). Revival will come, in large part, from believers who dedicate themselves to serving as God's end-time priests through prayer, fasting, worship, and giving.

This revival will reflect various facets of the person and work of the Holy Spirit. It will be characterized by healings, miracles, salvations, prosperity, and joy, as well as evangelization to ethnic groups who have never before heard the gospel. There will be supernatural activity all over the world. Spiritual doors and portals will open, and there will be an openness in people to receive the gospel. The church's apostles and prophets themselves are a type of portal because they will ignite this revival in the Spirit and open new territories for the kingdom.

I believe the end-time revival has already begun, which is why we are seeing a satanic backlash against Christians around the world. Previously, we discussed how believers in countries such as Malaysia, Iran, and China are suffering persecution. Let's look at some additional examples of Christians being oppressed. The persecution in China is relentless. Voice of the Martyrs reports that governmental authorities in Zhejiang province have sanctioned a new set of measures prohibiting baptism, changes in church locations, and growth in congregations. Among other restrictions, churches can't hold a bank account or receive donations from other countries.[35] A church in Nanjing, in Jiangsu province, that provided services for a thousand area Christians (a number that speaks of the revival the church is experiencing amid persecution) was demolished in the middle of the night. Believers who had gathered to worship were dragged out of the building, and some of them were beaten. These Christians knelt in front of their church, "crying and screaming," as governmental authorities tore down the building.

---

35. "China: New Measures Forbid Baptism," Voice of the Martyrs, November 6, 2019, https://vom.com.au/china-new-measures-forbid-baptism/.

This is just the latest in a series of Chinese church demolitions. An anonymous Nanjing pastor said he believes the government's motive is to destroy Christianity.

Since President Xi Jinping assumed power in 2013, he has instituted "religion with Chinese characteristics," a scheme to bring theology under government control. The Chinese government fears the spread of religion will undermine their power.[36]

Revival has also prompted great persecution of Christians in Laos, a country in Southeast Asia. In the north, whole districts have received Jesus. Some local authorities have declared that any person who converts to Christ no longer falls under their protection, and the believers are forced to leave the village. Anyone who wants to return must "perform a sacrificial ceremony to their ancestors and return to their old practices."[37] The dominant belief in that area is animism, the idea that all objects, places, and creatures have an essential spirit, making the human being equal to inanimate objects. The leaders are the shamans, who are thought to have influence over the world of evil and good spirits. Even in the midst of intense persecution, "the believers are faithfully committed to following Christ and do not deny their newfound faith."[38]

In Cuba, authorities have continually threatened a pastor who has been working on the reconstruction of churches damaged by a hurricane that hit the island in 2018. Although the damaged structures have been used for worship services for years, the government does not recognize church buildings built after the 1959 revolution. This pastor was also denied the right to register his car or put up a sign at his church. In order to continue repairs, he and other Christians have had to work at night, but even so, the pastor was threatened by a neighbor

36. "China: Nanjing Church Demolished," Voice of the Martyrs, November 28, 2019, https://vom.com.au/china-nanjing-church-demolished/.
37. "Persecution and Revival," Voice of the Martyrs, August 26, 2015, https://vom.com.au/persecution-and-revival/.
38. Ibid.

with a machete.[39] Despite such tribulations, revival has come to this Caribbean island and continues to grow.

Thus, while the end-time revival is global and joyful, it is also generating persecution. We must be ready to stand strong in our faith in the midst of opposition, just as believers in these nations have needed to.

WE CANNOT BE EFFECTIVE PREACHERS OF THE GOSPEL WITHOUT GOING THROUGH A SHAKING. THAT IS WHAT WILL CAUSE DIVINE REVIVAL.

Remember that there must be divine shakings before the gospel can be preached to the whole world. Human beings, by nature, tend to be easily distracted, losing their focus and forgetting their priorities. However, people seek God when they are in crisis. God will use these shakings to revive the church and pour out His Holy Spirit in a measure even greater than He did when the church began. The shakings will awaken believers to develop a deep relationship with God as they renew their commitment to praying, giving, and evangelizing.

This will be the last revival before the end of the age, and it will be massive. In the past, much of the church has taken revival for granted, not understanding its true purpose. Revival does not come simply so we can enjoy ourselves, warm the seats of our churches, and be insulated from the rest of the world. It comes to prompt us to repent and to empower us to bring people to the light of Christ so they can be saved. Some people want revival for their own benefit, without being concerned about others. It doesn't work that way. God's plan is not selfish or focused on individuals. True revival is for everyone. People's spiritual

---

39. "Cuba: Pastor Threatened for Repairing Churches," Voice of the Martyrs, March 14, 2019, https://vom.com.au/cuba-pastor-threatened-for-repairing-churches/.

ignorance and lack of revelation can cause them to miss out on revival and be excluded from the kingdom. Let's be wise!

We must understand that in the end-time revival, not everything will be revived. Anything that God judges will not be brought back to life. God will revive the people and ministries that are responsive to His Spirit and are ready to participate in His supernatural movement.

We need to be vigilant and not lose sight of the purpose of the end-time revival. Amid this awakening, God will choose His remnant from among all Christians on earth and identify these refined ones as the bride of Christ. They will serve as effective witnesses of the gospel, demonstrating supernatural power through miracles, signs, and wonders. I challenge you to walk soberly and righteously in holiness before God. May your passion be pleasing to Him.

> ## THE REMNANT BRIDE IS BEING REVIVED FOR THE LAST DAYS.

ACKNOWLEDGE THE REALITY OF HELL

In today's church, there is little acknowledgment of the reality of hell. We cannot effectively preach the gospel—or be motivated to do so—until we know, in the depths of our heart, that hell is real and that it is possible for people to end up there.

> *So it was that the beggar died, and was carried by the angels to Abraham's bosom. The rich man also died and was buried. And being in torments in Hades, he lifted up his eyes and saw Abraham afar off, and Lazarus in his bosom. Then he cried and said, "Father Abraham, have mercy on me, and send Lazarus that he may dip the tip of his finger in water and cool my tongue; for I am tormented in this flame."* (Luke 16:22–24)

Jesus was emphatic about the reality of hell. In fact, He spoke more about hell than He did about heaven. His advice for avoiding this place of punishment was also forceful and vivid with imagery: *"If your hand causes you to sin, cut it off. It is better for you to enter into life maimed, rather than having two hands, to go to hell, into the fire that shall never be quenched—where 'their worm does not die, and the fire is not quenched'"* (Mark 9:43–44).

Hell is a place of eternal punishment from which no one can escape. (See, for example, Matthew 23:33.) It was created for Satan and his rebellious angels, but the devil wants company. Therefore, he works day and night so that more and more people will end up there with him.

In 1979, a woman named Glenda Jackson had a vision of hell and saw terrible sights. She related how an angel took her into a bottomless place. The smell there was unbearable, and people were incessantly burning. Glenda was shocked to see former presidents, famous singers, and even preachers in that place.[40]

The greatest deceptions the devil tries to get the world to believe are that he does not exist and that hell is not real. You don't have to go to hell yourself to prove that it is real. I don't want to go to hell for anyone, nor do I want anyone to have to go to that place of torment. We know hell exists because Jesus said so and strongly warned us not to end up there. He gave His own life so that we could live with Him in heaven and not be condemned to eternal punishment. This is one of the reasons why I preach the gospel all over the world. I am ready to spread the good news of the kingdom *"in season and out of season"* (2 Timothy 4:2).

ANYONE WHO UNDERSTANDS THE REALITY OF HELL WILL TESTIFY TO OTHERS ABOUT JESUS.

---

40. "Our Guest Glenda Jackson," *Sid Roth One New Man TV*, February 19, 2015, http://www.onenewman.tv/2015/02/19/our-guest-glenda-jackson/.

DEVELOP A SENSE OF URGENCY

If we do not truly believe in the reality of hell, we will not feel an urgency to evangelize. We will think that we have all the time in the world to tell others about Jesus. Yet people without Christ are dying by the thousands every day! Because we know Jesus is coming back, we must evangelize as if there is no tomorrow. Paul conveyed this sense of urgency in a letter to his spiritual son Timothy, a portion of which I quoted above: *"I charge you therefore before God and the Lord Jesus Christ, who will judge the living and the dead at His appearing and His kingdom: Preach the word! Be ready in season and out of season. Convince, rebuke, exhort, with all longsuffering and teaching"* (2 Timothy 4:1–2).

Think about this: if you were to die tomorrow, which place would rejoice, heaven or hell? What would happen to the people around you if they were to die tomorrow? We must call others to salvation with the knowledge that there will be a final judgment. Today, we are seeing very few conversions in our churches because the "gospel" people are hearing is only about receiving blessings. They are not being told they are in danger of judgment and are in critical need of salvation.

Again, we need to have a sense of urgency about calling the lost to receive Jesus because we do not know what tomorrow will bring. Suppose someone visits your church for the first time next Sunday. You might think you will see them the following week to talk to them about their spiritual state. But who knows whether they will come back to your church or even live to see another day? That visit might be their last chance to hear the word of truth and make a commitment to Christ. It doesn't matter if someone is educated or uneducated, rich or poor, famous or obscure, popular or unpopular. If they don't know Jesus, they are headed to hell unless they repent and receive Him as Lord and Savior, making a commitment to follow Him.

We must populate heaven and depopulate hell! The next time you see someone who doesn't know Jesus, imagine them burning in the eternal fires of hell. Picture them being tormented day and night. You may be the only one who can pull that person out of the fire through the power of God's Spirit. You must see people as God sees them and value them as He does.

I encourage you to go out into the world and win people for the Lord. There is someone in your sphere of influence who has asked God for a sign, and if you will tell them about Jesus, they will believe. Supernatural evidence follows those who "go." (See Mark 16:15–18.) I activate you to go to people in your family, neighborhood, city, and beyond to preach the true gospel of the kingdom with the demonstration of God's power! You have been anointed to be an effective witness for Christ. Remember that the sign of Jesus's second coming is the preaching of the gospel. If you go out and preach now, you will be hastening the coming of the Lord.

PROCLAIM THE GOOD NEWS

The signs are evident. *"He who has ears to hear, let him hear!"* (Mark 4:9). Nature itself cries out for the return of the Lord and the manifestation of the children of God. (See Romans 8:19.) After being refined and purified, the remnant is called to preach the good news of the kingdom everywhere during the end-time revival that is coming upon the earth in this generation. We must do this with a sense of urgency, in season and out of season, keenly aware of the reality of hell for those who do not believe.

Christ is coming soon! This is no time for hesitancy or doubt. This is no time to sleep, but to watch, pray, and proclaim the good news because the Spirit and the bride say, "Come, Lord Jesus!" Do you say the same? Will you join in the cry of the Spirit and the bride, calling for the imminent coming of the Son of God? *Maranatha!* Come, Lord Jesus!

SUMMARY

+ Jesus's disciples asked Him three questions concerning the last days: *"When will these things be? And what will be the sign of Your coming, and of the end of the age?"* (Matthew 24:3).

+ A sign is not an end in itself, but rather points to something or someone. It is "something material or external that stands for or signifies something spiritual."

+ Every sign from God points back to Him.

+ All the signs that Jesus revealed point to His appearing, His coming, and the end of the world.

+ The apostles and prophets are God's means of bringing revelation to the church concerning the end-time signs disclosed by the Holy Spirit.

+ Many prophecies concerning Christ's coming have been fulfilled in the past century, and prophecies continue to be fulfilled in our day. It is happening before our eyes.

+ The sign of Christ's appearing is the shaking of all things, which will occur in stages: a preliminary shaking, an intermediate shaking (which we are currently going through), and a final shaking, which we are approaching.

+ God will shake every dimension and sphere of life—the heavens, the earth, the seas, the weather, nations, governments, institutions, the world economy, families, individuals, and even Satan and his demons—and only what is established in Christ will remain standing.

+ The sign of Jesus's second coming and the end of the age is the preaching of the gospel throughout the world.

+ For us to preach the gospel effectively, we must be part of the end-time revival, acknowledge the reality of hell, and develop a sense of urgency to reach the lost before it is too late.

SIGNS OF THE TIMES TESTIMONIES

MANIFESTATIONS OF END-TIME REVIVAL

End-time revival is a telling sign of Christ's coming. The following are glimpses of what is happening around the world as King Jesus Ministry and the churches under our spiritual covering preach the gospel and experience the prophesied revival.

In his ministry, Apostle Shammah Apwam of South Africa has seen thousands of Muslims come to Christ. Here is his testimony about how God is moving:

> I am one of the leaders taking part in the revival that has been released over our nation. Since 2011, we have touched every major city with miracle crusades, activating pastors and leaders in the supernatural. In every city where we travel, we experience strong satanic opposition in the form of witchcraft and religiosity, but the Lord always gives us the victory. We are seeing a massive movement of the Holy Spirit that is reaching thousands of souls every year. Here are some examples of what God is doing.
>
> I met a young Muslim man who had given his life to Jesus but was suffering unbearable pain in his testicles. He had undergone two unsuccessful surgeries, and he came to us asking for help. Even though he knew his family would reject him, he was baptized as a believer. After his baptism, all the pain left his body. During one crusade, I ministered to a young woman who had been suffering for five years from an infection, which had developed as a complication of a Caesarean section. The wound was constantly oozing. We prayed for her, and the oozing stopped. She went to the doctor and was declared healed! Another time, we learned that a member of our church was stuck in a collapsed mine. The church interceded for him, and he was rescued after three days, safe and sound. As soon as he was rescued, the mine completely collapsed. A man came to us with lung disease after

having smoked for thirty years. We prayed for him, and three days later, his doctor told him that his lungs were as clean as if he had never smoked. We heard about a young man who had been in a coma for eight days and was about to be disconnected from the life-support machines. We prayed for him, and he immediately regained consciousness. The doctors were shocked at his recovery.

We are training leaders in evangelism and in other areas of ministry, and we have a 24-7 prayer chain. We know that we are seeing the outpouring of the Holy Spirit in the last days—that this is the time of the greatest harvest of souls ever seen. So, it is time to return to the sea and cast out our nets, with massive evangelism that is accompanied by great miracles, signs, and wonders for this last mile of the church's existence on earth.

Apostle Edgar Ortuño of Ministerio Internacional Centro de Vida Sobrenatural (Supernatural Life Center International Ministry) in Bolivia provides spiritual covering for more than sixty churches throughout Latin America. The revival in his country is affecting all spheres of society, and he is witnessing many miracles and signs in his huge evangelistic crusades.

We have seen the glory of God descend upon our nation. Our ministry has influenced pastors, ministries, governmental authorities, businessmen, workers, and farmers. We are seeing miracles, conversions, deliverances, and prosperity like never before. More than three hundred and fifty thousand people attended our last supernatural gathering. Some of the miracles we have seen include people having money appear in their purses and bank accounts, people being completely healed of terminal cancer, and people becoming free of pain and regaining movement after having surgery involving metal implants, with the implants totally disappearing. One healing that particularly stood out to me was that of Raul Flores. He had rashes and sores all over his body so that he was unable to move about or even walk. We prayed for him, and within ten minutes, his skin was clean and healthy.

The biggest attack against our ministry has been a spirit of religiosity. Some of our brothers in Christ have taken it upon themselves to defame us. We have also been attacked by people who adhere to the socialist and communist culture in our country. The hardest obstacles have been political, followed by witchcraft and occultism. But the greater the resistance, the greater the support God gives us.

All the signs are intensifying, showing us that the coming of our beloved Christ is closer than ever. This has brought a sense of urgency to consecrate ourselves, to daily renew ourselves in God's Spirit, and to prepare, as members of the remnant, to extend His kingdom in power. We feel that there is no time to lose and this is a period of revival and great harvest. Therefore, we have made evangelism a way of life. We conduct both mass evangelism in public places and one-on-one witnessing, with new believers from these contacts making up 98 percent of the members in our church. As a result of the most recent supernatural gathering presided over by our apostle, Guillermo Maldonado, in three months we evangelized three hundred and ninety thousand people, to whom we gave close spiritual attention and care.

We have also received supernatural provision for each of our events. Although we had no money, God supplied our needs, and we have never had any financial troubles. We understand that this movement is not a natural work. It is not about strategies or methods; rather, it is a spiritual battle. Persistent prayer is what sustains us and gives us the victory.

We recently ministered in Pakistan, during which we visited the city of Karachi. Although Karachi is considered one of the most dangerous places in the world, we went there because the Lord spoke to me during a fast and commissioned me to go into the heart of this city to preach the power of Jesus Christ. Here is a report from one of the participants in our meetings:

> On the first day, a service was held for seven thousand influential leaders of Pakistan. The next night, more than a million people gathered outside one of the country's largest stadiums. The number of attendees was verified by the Karachi police and the Pakistani government's satellite service. This monumental event was the largest open-air Christian gathering in the history of Pakistan, and 95 percent of the attendees were not Christians but Muslims. More than nine hundred thousand souls came to know the saving power of Jesus Christ. Signs, miracles, and wonders were manifested among the people, with thousands healed of diseases.
>
> Apostle Maldonado testified, "There was no choir or music, so I taught about the supernatural without a spiritual atmosphere. I had to use raw authority, and God began to work. In that kind of atmosphere, you cannot operate by faith or anointing. It was God's sovereign manifestation of His glory that brought the miracles and deliverances. According to the government of Pakistan, 97 percent of the 190 million Pakistanis are Muslims, while only 3 percent are Christians. We announced this event on Karachi television, and people attended because we declared there would be miracles. The moment I set foot on the platform, I felt God's love and presence. I know that Pakistan was transformed forever."
>
> At the leaders' event, there were many miracles, including blind people seeing, deaf people hearing, and paralyzed people walking by the power of God. The Lord has been faithful in all He has done for our city, and we are eternally grateful for what He has continued to do in His supernatural power.

Noé Banegas from Tegucigalpa, Honduras, is a youth leader at the Centro Cristiano Renovación Internacional (International Renovation Christian Center), under Apostle Jorge Suazo, a member of our ministry network. God is using him to introduce young people to His supernatural power. In this end-time revival, Noé is holding meetings in cities, and people are being healed and transformed by the power of God.

My testimony is about the supernatural movement that has awakened many young people in my country. A number of us at our church were activated in God's power through King Jesus Ministry, and we decided to provoke a spiritual movement, so we prayed to God for this to happen. We went through biblical training and received spiritual impartations, and when we applied what we had learned and received, changes began to occur!

Today, we are going forth in a movement that is reaching Honduras for God. We have learned to lose our fear and minister in the streets. The young people of our church have gone into various cities with worship, praise, prayer, and evangelism, creating a heavenly atmosphere in the central plazas. People in these cities who were thirsty for God, sick, and in spiritual bondage have stopped by or walked near our gathering places. There, they have encountered God, and their bonds have been broken. People have been set free, right in the streets!

One time, in a square in Tegucigalpa, we were worshipping, and the evangelists were approaching people. A young woman who was passing by stopped to see what was happening. At that moment, she was broken before God. No one touched her or did anything else to her. For years, she had been carrying resentment in her heart against her mother. She stated that she could feel God's love and said, "I don't know, but I want to forgive my mom." Coincidentally, the mother was there, too, among the people, and the miracle of forgiveness occurred. Another woman was bent over and unable to move. She was ministered to by one of the evangelists, and immediately, all her pain left. We have seen young people leave gangs, become freed from drug addiction, and much more. As we are out in the streets, they come to us. We give them a prophetic word from God and show them His power, and they give their lives to Christ. They become free! And then they, too, join this movement, ministering to other people in the same way!

The media in Honduras has put a spotlight on the supernatural revolution occurring among the youth, featuring us on television. As a result, many Hondurans have heard about this movement. We young Christians are even influencing the government. A few months ago, some legislators made an attempt to pass a law approving abortion. A large group of us gathered to worship God and pray in a public area in Tegucigalpa on the same day the law was being discussed in Congress. We decreed that this law would not be passed; we proclaimed life and not death. Other young people who were in favor of abortion came to intimidate us, but we continued to worship and pray. In the afternoon, the bill was annulled! It is an undeniable fact that this supernatural movement has brought about changes in our ministry, our families, and our nation.

CHAPTER 5

END-TIME SIGNS

But as the days of Noah were, so also will the coming of the Son of Man be. For as in the days before the flood, they were eating and drinking, marrying and giving in marriage, until the day that Noah entered the ark, and did not know until the flood came and took them all away, so also will the coming of the Son of Man be.
—Matthew 24:37–39

Who will be ready for Jesus's appearing and His second coming? Noah preached for 120 years, yet only he and his immediate family members believed God's warning and were saved from the worldwide flood. Noah was the voice of God for his generation, but the people did not care to hear the message. They did not want to receive the prophetic word. Noah's generation was marked by hardness of heart and spiritual deafness, much like today's generation.

Jesus's disciples asked Him about the sign of His coming and the close of the age (see Matthew 2:3) because they understood that all seasons are identified by signs. Keep in mind that a sign is not an end in itself but rather points to something or someone. A biblical sign always represents a higher spiritual reality. All the signs that Jesus revealed point to His appearing and His coming.

In the physical world, we recognize the transition between seasons by changes that occur in nature, such as a substantial drop or rise in temperature, the departure or return of migratory birds, the withering or blooming of leaves on trees, and the emergence of young plants from the ground or the development of fully mature plants for harvest. In the same way, we can identify which spiritual season and time we are living in by the signs we see around us and in the world at large.

THE SIGNS OF THE END TIMES ARE RELATED TO THREE SPECIFIC AREAS: PROPHECY, THE FEASTS OF THE LORD, AND THE SECOND COMING OF JESUS.

We have noted that Christ's second coming will happen several years after the rapture of the remnant. The second coming coincides with the end of an era and the end of time. However, remember that this will not yet be the fullness of all times; the second coming will inaugurate the millennial age, in which Christ will rule over the earth before the final battle against Satan.

Most of the end-time signs have already been fulfilled. However, we need to recognize the common characteristic of the signs that are currently being fulfilled (or soon will be): they are intensifying. God's judgment on mankind's rebellion, sin, and wickedness is coming to the earth. The signs are clear. When God brings something to an end, it will be judged, and that is what is happening before our eyes. The present earth is coming to a close, and God is judging mankind through disruptions in the natural world, among other distresses. (See, for example, Psalm 148:8; Jeremiah 10:13.)

Many people easily recognize that God is a God of love and forgiveness who gives us the opportunity to repent of our sins. He is the

One who came to earth to die for us so that, if we return to Him, we can receive His mercy. However, there is another facet to God that is lesser known to many people but just as real: God is a God of wrath and judgment against sin. The moment mankind's cup of iniquity and sin overflows and is poured out, God will judge the world, just as He did the cities of Sodom and Gomorrah in the Old Testament. (See Genesis 19.)

> **WHEN GOD BRINGS SOMETHING TO AN END, IT WILL BE JUDGED.**

SIGNS OF THE TIMES

End-time signs are heaven's billboards announcing Jesus's appearing and second coming. In this chapter, we will review prophetic signs described in the books of Daniel, Matthew, Luke, and 1 Timothy. These signs are not necessarily the only indicators of the last days, but they are the most significant. Although we have explored some of these signs in previous chapters, I have also included them here so that we can understand the scope of the divine warnings. God is speaking to us, and we must respond to His prophetic word.

DECEPTION

Four times in Matthew 24, Jesus warns believers against being deceived: "*And Jesus answered and said to them: 'Take heed that no one deceives you. For many will come in My name, saying, "I am the Christ," and will deceive many'*" (Matthew 24:4–5). "*Then many false prophets will rise up and deceive many*" (verse 11). "*For false christs and false prophets will rise and show great signs and wonders to deceive, if possible, even the elect*" (verse 24).

The end-time sign of deception is very apparent today. Deceit is the spirit of this age. Even in the church, many people are being deceived by false gospels and empty promises, and they are turning away from the faith.

Deception is a perversion of truth. A Barna study looked at how the beliefs of Americans identified as "practicing Christians" have been affected by other worldviews, such as New Spirituality (one of whose views is that "all people pray to the same god or spirit, no matter what name they use for that spiritual being"), postmodernism, Marxism, and secularism. Among those surveyed, "61% agree with ideas rooted in New Spirituality, 54% resonate with postmodernist views, 36% accept ideas associated with Marxism, and 29% believe ideas based on secularism."[41]

In today's culture, it is easy to become swept up in ideologies that are contrary to the Scriptures unless we carefully weigh these ideas against sound biblical doctrine. Except for the remnant of believers who will be watching and praying, everyone will be deceived by the devil and accept his lies. We cannot be deceived unless we believe a lie. Deception occurs when we either are ignorant of, or reject, the truth.

Paul was careful to teach Christians the truth in Christ Jesus and to warn them to hold fast to what they had been taught. He wrote to Timothy, "*Hold fast the pattern of sound words which you have heard from me, in faith and love which are in Christ Jesus*" (2 Timothy 1:13). And he wrote to the Thessalonians, "*You are witnesses, and God also, how devoutly and justly and blamelessly we behaved ourselves among you who believe; as you know how we exhorted, and comforted, and charged every one of you, as a father does his own children*" (1 Thessalonians 2:10–11).

In chapter 4, we noted other serious distortions of the true gospel. One of these distortions is the belief that you can go to heaven even though you continue to live in sin. If you hold this belief, you are deceived. This idea is a perversion of the truths that God is merciful

---

41. "Competing Worldviews Influence Today's Christians," Barna Group, May 9, 2017, https://www.barna.com/research/competing-worldviews-influence-todays-christians/. Note: practicing Christians are defined as those who "go to church at least monthly and consider their faith very important in their life."

and Jesus understands our weaknesses. The reality is that we will only go to heaven if we repent of our sin and turn from our wrongdoing, seeking to lead a holy life. We also discussed the false belief of "super grace" theology, which says that once you are saved, it is impossible to lose your salvation by falling away from God. It is true that we are saved by grace and that our salvation is eternal because Jesus paid the ultimate and final penalty for our sin on the cross. Yet it is possible to reject that salvation by ignoring the price Jesus paid and by living in any manner we desire, not allowing God to transform us. If you are a Christian, you must *"bear fruits worthy of repentance"* (Matthew 3:8).

WE CANNOT BE DECEIVED UNLESS WE BELIEVE A LIE. DECEPTION OCCURS WHEN WE REJECT THE TRUTH.

FALSE PROPHETS

"For many will come in My name, saying, 'I am the Christ,' and will deceive many.... Then many false prophets will rise up and deceive many" (Matthew 24:5, 11). A false prophet is someone who has a spirit of impersonation, deception, or pretense. Many false prophets and false messiahs have arisen throughout history, deceiving numerous people, and we will see more such counterfeits in the end times. The following are a few examples.

In the August 2017 issue of *National Geographic*, journalist and photographer Jonas Bendiksen describes how he set out to discover, meet, and interview people who have proclaimed themselves to be the Messiah or the "Second Coming of Christ" in order to study their doctrines and meet their disciples. In his article, Bendiksen reports on his encounters with five of these "Christs." The first is a man in Brazil known as "INRI Cristo." The second is a man in Eshowe, South Africa, who is known as "The King of Kings, The Lord of Lords, Jesus." The third is a man in the forests of Siberia who goes by the name of "Vissarion," or "The Christ of Siberia." This individual has at least five thousand followers who live together and have even built their own society, including schools and churches. The fourth is a man who lives in Zambia. He has several names, including "Jesus of Kitwe" and "Parent Rock of the World," but his disciples call him "Jesus." The final self-proclaimed messiah was a man (since deceased) in Japan who called himself "Jesus Matayoshi" or "The One True God." He was campaigning for a seat in the Japanese parliament with the goal of becoming the secretary general of the United Nations and "instituting God's will on earth."[42]

If you encounter any person who claims to be the Messiah, remember that Jesus Christ said, "*I am the way, the truth, and the life. No one comes to the Father except through Me*" (John 14:6). When the true Jesus appears for His remnant, it will be a quick appearance, like lightning. And when He returns in the second coming, everyone on earth will see and acknowledge Him. He will not merely have pockets of followers here and there in the world. Make sure you know what Jesus has said about His return so you won't be misled.

WARS AND RUMORS OF WARS

"*And you will hear of wars and rumors of wars. See that you are not troubled; for all these things must come to pass, but the end is not yet*" (Matthew 24:6). "*But when you hear of wars and commotions, do not be terrified; for these things must come to pass first, but the end will not come immediately*" (Luke 21:9). Over the centuries, wars have been fought for various reasons: to gain dominance, territory, or resources; to force others to submit to a particular ideology or religion; and much more. Waging war is costly in numerous ways. Wars leave behind death, deficits, poverty, disease, and material destruction.

---

42. Jonas Bendiksen, "Meet Five Men Who All Think They're the Messiah," *National Geographic*, July 2017, https://www.nationalgeographic.com/magazine/2017/08/new-messiahs-jesus-christ-second-coming-photos/.

Today, through the media, we receive frequent reports about conflicts across the globe as well as rumors of conflicts. Such clashes are a sign of the end times. The website Wars in the World provides a list of current conflicts. As of this writing, within thirty countries in Africa alone, there are 274 conflicts. These represent ethnic clashes, frequent armed conflicts between Muslims and Christians, warfare against rebel groups, civil wars in Libya, wars against Islamic militants in Nigeria and Somalia, and much more. Within sixteen countries in Asia, there are 183 conflicts involving militia, guerrilla, terrorist, separatist, or anarchist groups. The hot spots are Afghanistan, Burma-Myanmar, Pakistan, the Philippines, and Thailand.

In Europe, within ten countries, there are 82 conflicts. Some of the worst fighting is in the Russian Federation (Chechnya and Dagestan) and in Ukraine. In the Middle East, within seven countries, there are 261 conflicts, with the hottest places being Iraq, Israel, Syria, and Yemen. In the Americas, within seven countries, there are 32 conflicts involving drug cartel, terrorist, separatist, and anarchist groups. The hot spots are Colombia and Mexico. In total, there are 69 countries immersed in conflicts involving 839 groups.[43]

NATION RISING AGAINST NATION

"For nation will rise against nation, and kingdom against kingdom" (Matthew 24:7). The Greek word translated "nation" here is *ethnos*, one of whose meanings is "a tribe, race, or people group." This is the term from which the English word *ethnic* is derived. Jesus indicated that in the end times, we would see races and ethnic groups in conflict with one another. Today, we are seeing clashes involving blacks versus whites, whites versus Asians, Asians versus blacks, Hispanics versus other Hispanics, Hindus versus Muslims, Shiites versus Sunnis, Arabs versus Jews, and a number of other groups. Many of the conflicts that lead to war result from racial animosity. In these last days, we are bound to see racism increase more and more around the world.

---

43. "List of Ongoing Conflicts," Wars in the World, May 29, 2020, https://www.warsintheworld.com/?page=static1258254223.

JESUS INDICATED THAT IN THE END TIMES, WE WOULD SEE RACES AND ETHNIC GROUPS IN CONFLICT WITH ONE ANOTHER.

FAMINE AND PESTILENCE

"And there will be famines, pestilences, and earthquakes in various places" (Matthew 24:7). *"And there will be…famines and pestilences; and there will be fearful sights and great signs from heaven"* (Luke 21:11). The United Nations uses the following criteria to define famine: "At least 20 per cent of households in an area face extreme food shortages with a limited ability to cope; acute malnutrition rates exceed 30 per cent; and the death rate exceeds two persons per day per 10,000 persons."[44]

What are the causes of famine? One nonprofit group that focuses on global poverty explains, "Famine looks like a lack of food, and most people think it is brought on by a drought, a war, or an outbreak of disease.… But famines are usually caused by multiple factors, compounded by poor (or even intentionally bad) policy decisions that make people vulnerable.[45]

The United Nations' July 2019 report on hunger stated that an estimated 820 million people do not have enough to eat. This means that one out of every nine people in the world suffers from hunger. That was the third consecutive year the number of hungry had increased. In 2018, the number was 811 million.[46] Thus, there seems to be a new trend in which, after years of decline, global hunger is rising. And this assessment was given before the COVID-19 emergency. With all the repercussions

---

44. "When a Food Security Crisis Becomes a Famine," UN News, July 21, 2011, https://news.un.org/en/story/2011/07/382342-when-food-security-crisis-becomes-famine.
45. Chris Hufstader, "What Is Famine, and How Can We Stop It?" May 14, 2020, https://www.oxfamamerica.org/explore/stories/what-is-famine-and-how-can-we-stop-it/.
46. "Over 820 Million People Suffering from Hunger; New UN Report Reveals Stubborn Realities of 'Immense' Global Challenge," UN News, July 15, 2019, https://news.un.org/en/story/2019/07/1042411.

from that disease, "the economic crisis and disruption of the food supply could push an additional half billion people into poverty."[47]

We need to be aware that in the last days, a famine is coming to the earth that will be so great it will require the same anointing of wisdom God gave Joseph in the Old Testament. Joseph received a revelation of impending famine and was able to implement a plan to supply the nation of Egypt and many surrounding areas with grain during that distressing time. This plan even preserved the line of the Messiah from starvation. Joseph provided grain and shelter for his father, Jacob, and for all his brothers, including Judah. Because famine is a sign of the end times, we must recognize that there is a demonic strategy behind it designed to steal souls from the kingdom by causing people to die prematurely.

There is a strong connection between famine and drought, and we have noted that weather patterns around the world are becoming more severe. What we are experiencing with hurricanes, tornadoes, heat waves, heavy snowfall, el Niño, and la Niña is clear evidence that climate change is occurring. There have never been such extreme high and low temperatures and as many hurricanes with high-speed winds. Jesus obviously anticipated this development: *And there will be signs in the sun, in the moon, and in the stars; and on the earth distress of nations, with perplexity, the sea and the waves roaring* (Luke 21:25).

The World Meteorological Organization (WMO) describes the El Niño/Southern Oscillation as a natural phenomenon characterized by "fluctuating ocean temperatures in the central and eastern equatorial Pacific, coupled with changes in the atmosphere," with "associated hazards such as heavy rains, floods and drought."[48] With this description, it is not difficult to understand why the phenomenon has become so threatening and why its ravages will grow in the years to come.

---

47. Hufstader, "What Is Famine?"
48. "El Niño/La Niña Update," World Meteorological Organization, https://public.wmo.int/en/our-mandate/climate/el-ni%C3%B1ola-ni%C3%B1a-update.

In addition to *"famines,"* Luke 21:11 talks about *"pestilences."* Included under this term would be epidemics and diseases that affect society over time. Every year, the World Health Organization reports outbreaks of epidemics that occur around the globe. In 2019 alone, the organization reported 111 outbreaks of various diseases, such as hantavirus, measles, Ebola, yellow fever, poliomyelitis, dengue fever, Zika virus, and an epidemic of flesh-eating insects, among many others. In 2018, there were 91 outbreaks. In 2017, there were 98. We have seen a total of 1,159 outbreaks of serious diseases, many of them infectious and viral, over a period of ten years.[49]

The recent Ebola outbreak in the Democratic Republic of the Congo has been going on since 2018 and may finally be under control. It has infected 3,500 people and killed more than 2,200. The deadliest Ebola outbreak occurred in West Africa from 2014 to 2016. It "infected and killed multiple times more people than had been infected and killed by all previous Ebola outbreaks combined."[50]

According to the World Health Organization, seasonal flu, or influenza, "is a serious global health threat that impacts all countries: every year, there are an estimated 1 billion cases, 3–5 million severe cases, and 290,000–650,000 influenza-related respiratory deaths worldwide."[51] Of course, since the end of 2019, the world has been reeling from the devastating, wide-ranging effects of the coronavirus pandemic. As of late June 2020, there were 8.7 million cases worldwide, with more than 460,000 deaths.[52] National economies and the global marketplace were greatly affected. The World Bank reported, "The baseline forecast envisions a 5.2 percent contraction in global GDP in 2020, using market exchange

---

49. See "Emergencies Preparedness, Response," World Health Organization, https://www.who.int/csr/don/en/.
50. Helen Branswell, "Second Deadliest Ebola Outbreak on Record Is Days from Being Declared Over," *Stat*, June 22, 2020, https://www.statnews.com/2020/06/22/second-deadliest-ebola-outbreak-on-record-is-days-from-being-declared-over/.
51. "Global Influenza Strategy 2019–2030," World Health Organization, https://www.who.int/influenza/Global_Influenza_Strategy_2019_2030_Summary_English.pdf?ua=1.
52. "Coronavirus Disease (COVID-19) Situation Report–153," World Health Organization, June 21, 2020, https://www.who.int/docs/default-source/coronaviruse/situation-reports/20200621-covid-19-sitrep-153.

rate weights—the deepest global recession in decades."[53] Actual and potential socioeconomic effects include challenges to fields such as agriculture; petroleum and oil; manufacturing; education; finance; healthcare and pharmaceutical; hospitality, tourism, and aviation; real estate and housing; sports; the food sector; and family dynamics.[54]

The sign of pestilence is definitely here!

EARTHQUAKES

"And there will be…earthquakes in various places" (Matthew 24:7). "And there will be great earthquakes in various places" (Luke 21:11). As mentioned in chapter 4 of this book, between the years 2000 and 2019, there were twenty-four earthquakes measuring 8 or higher on the Richter scale. I won't expand on this topic here because we covered it previously. But as the time of Jesus's return draws nearer, we can expect "great earthquakes" causing much destruction.

PERSECUTION OF THE CHURCH

"Then they will deliver you up to tribulation and kill you, and you will be hated by all nations for My name's sake" (Matthew 24:9). "But before all these things, they will lay their hands on you and persecute you, delivering you up to the synagogues and prisons. You will be brought before kings and rulers for My name's sake" (Luke 21:12). As mentioned previously, one sign of the end times and the coming of the Lord for His bride is the persecution of the church. Although we have discussed this topic in some detail already, it is important for us to understand what this will mean for Christians. We will see more oppression against believers than we have ever seen before, including in countries where such persecution has not occurred much in the past. For example, various governments have legalized sinful behaviors, and they have begun to pressure or penalize

53. "The Global Economic Outlook During the COVID-19 Pandemic: A Changed World," The World Bank, June 8, 2020, https://www.worldbank.org/en/news/feature/2020/06/08/the-global-economic-outlook-during-the-covid-19-pandemic-a-changed-world.
54. Maria Nicola and others, "The Socio-Economic Implications of the Coronavirus Pandemic (COVID-19): A Review," National Center for Biotechnology Information: Elsevier Public Health Emergency Collection, June 2020, https://www.ncbi.nlm.nih.gov/pmc/articles/PMC7162753/.

Christians if they don't comply with the corresponding new laws. This type of persecution will become more frequent.

As noted in earlier chapters, in some countries, believers are already suffering intense persecution. The following are some additional examples. Voice of the Martyrs reported that "nine Iranian Christians were sentenced to five years in prison for 'acting against national security' for their participation in a home church in Rasht."[55] In Egypt, a court sentenced a Coptic Christian to three years in prison. "Abdo Adel Bebawy, 43, was accused in July of publishing a post on his Facebook page that insulted Islam. In his post, Adel had compared Islam's prophet, Muhammad, with Jesus…. Following his arrest, a mob attacked houses owned by Copts and the situation has remained tense ever since."[56]

I myself have experienced persecution by false brothers and religious leaders who rejected the Holy Spirit and His work. But many pastors are being thrown into prison by their governments for simply preaching Jesus and speaking against sin. Others have been killed for the cause of Christ. Pray for these persecuted believers around the world and remain strong in your faith.

OFFENSES

"And then many will be offended, will betray one another, and will hate one another" (Matthew 24:10). Why do many people leave their churches? A major reason is that they have been offended in one way or another. One Barna Group study made this surprising discovery: 61 percent of the unchurched in America are self-identified Christians. Another Barna study among unchurched adults showed that "nearly four out of every ten non-churchgoing Americans (37%) said they avoid churches because of negative past experiences in churches or with church people."[57]

55. "Iran: Nine Christians Sentenced to Five Year Imprisonment," Voice of the Martyrs, October 24, 2019, https://vom.com.au/iran-nine-christians-sentenced-to-five-year-imprisonment/.
56. "Egypt: Facebook Post Leads to Imprisonment," Voice of the Martyrs, December 19, 2018, https://vom.com.au/egypt-facebook-post-leads-to-three-years-imprisonment/.
57. "Millions of Unchurched Adults Are Christians Hurt by Churches but Can Be Healed of the Pain," Barna Group, April 12, 2010, https://www.barna.com/research/millions-of-unchurched-adults-are-christians-hurt-by-churches-but-can-be-healed-of-the-pain/.

Many believers have been sinned against and hurt by their fellow Christians. While that hurt is real, God calls us to forgive others and to let go of our resentment against them. Taking offense and holding on to grudges is often related to spiritual immaturity. Those who are immature are often quick to feel insulted. People can become offended over the smallest matters. I have seen numerous people turn from their faith in Christ because of just one offense. I don't want you to fulfill this end-time prophecy by becoming one of the *"many [who] will be offended"*! Develop spiritual maturity and do not allow offense to rob you of your inheritance as a child of God at Christ's coming. You need to forgive anyone who has wronged you and overcome the pain because you will not be taken to heaven in the rapture if you carry an offense in your heart. If someone has hurt you, this is the time to forgive them and release any bitterness.

DO NOT ALLOW OFFENSE TO ROB YOU OF YOUR INHERITANCE AS A CHILD OF GOD AT CHRIST'S COMING.

LAWLESSNESS, OR INIQUITY

"And because lawlessness will abound, the love of many will grow cold" (Matthew 24:12). Lawlessness is equivalent to rebellion, and rebellion is a mark of the antichrist spirit. Our generation is characterized by such anarchism, especially among the youth. There are people who do not want to submit to any form of authority. For them, the law—whether human law or heavenly law—means control, and therefore they defy the law. This rejection of moral parameters ultimately leads them to reject God Himself.

Sometimes, human laws can be lawless. As we noted earlier, in many countries, sinful behaviors have been legalized. For example, abortion and same-sex marriage are permitted. In public schools, children are taught sex education promoting the idea that homosexuality is acceptable. Please do not misunderstand what I am saying. I love all people, including homosexuals, lesbians, and women who have had abortions. God loves them! But that does not mean He loves the sins they have committed. The same is true for all of us. Only God's Spirit can reveal to people their sin and lead them to repent so they can be forgiven, be set free, and live as God created them to. Therefore, we must endeavor to lead others to Christ.

LOVE GROWING COLD

"And because lawlessness will abound, the love of many will grow cold" (Matthew 24:12). This sign of the end times is connected to the sign of offenses. I know many people who used to be on fire for God, faithfully serving Him, but now they have turned away from the Lord. Some of these people saw so much sin, wickedness, and hypocritical behavior within the church that they gave up and left. Others were betrayed or rejected by another person, and as a result, they became disillusioned and bitter. In both of these situations, the individuals' love for God and other people grew cold. They abandoned their relationship with the Father and began living according to the values of the world. There are others whose love has grown cold because they did not know how to cultivate their relationship with God or did not take the time to do so. They never learned how to watch and pray. As you read this book, if you are drifting from your faith, the Holy Spirit is calling you to return to Christ, your *"first love"* (Revelation 2:4). None of us has an excuse to let the negative behavior of others influence us, allowing their mistakes or evil deeds to cause us to forsake our devotion to God. Don't become a statistic! Return wholeheartedly to the Lord and let His love and presence fill you again.

THE PREACHING OF THE GOSPEL IN ALL THE WORLD

"And this gospel of the kingdom will be preached in all the world as a witness to all the nations, and then the end will come" (Matthew 24:14). In the previous chapter, we talked about the gospel being preached to the whole world as the primary sign of Jesus's second coming, the final sign that indicates the end of the age. I will not spend much time on this point, either, because we have already covered it at length. I will only add that if you are part of the remnant that prepares the way for Christ's appearance in glory, you must take part in world evangelization with a sense of urgency.

FEAR

Jesus told us that people's hearts would "[fail] *them from fear and the expectation of those things which are coming on the earth, for the powers of the heavens will be shaken*" (Luke 21:26). In these end times, the increased presence of the dark side of the supernatural, or the demonic, on the earth will cause many people to fear. Today, atrocities are taking place that have not occurred before; wickedness has multiplied to such an extent that many people no longer experience peace. A Pew Research Center survey found that seven out of ten American teenagers see anxiety and depression as one of the biggest problems among their peers.[58]

Some countries experience much violence and unrest. People around the world are filled with fear and dread because they anticipate the arrival of disaster, whether through the effects of global warming and climate change, economic crises and catastrophes, water or food shortages, terrorist acts, the violence of drug cartels, or something else.

Many people's fears are based on genuine problems they are facing, although fear is not a helpful response to them. However, people are also suffering from unfounded apprehensions that come from evil spirits for the malevolent purpose of making them faint with fear. "*The thief does not come except to steal, and to kill, and to destroy*" (John 10:10).

---

58. Juliana Menasce Horowitz and Nikki Graf, "Most U.S. Teens See Anxiety and Depression as a Major Problem Among Their Peers," Pew Research Center, Washington, D.C., February 20, 2019, https://www.pewsocialtrends.org/2019/02/20/most-u-s-teens-see-anxiety-and-depression-as-a-major-problem-among-their-peers/.

These people imagine frightening scenarios. They suffer confusion, loss of appetite, panic attacks, anxiety, insomnia, torment, and diseases. Then, their fearful reactions to these imagined threats attract even more demonic spirits.

Whatever anxieties you are facing, remember that God is greater than all our fears and that fear does not come from Him. *"For God has not given us a spirit of fear, but of power and of love and of a sound mind"* (2 Timothy 1:7).

AN INCREASE IN KNOWLEDGE

"But you, Daniel, shut up the words, and seal the book until the time of the end; many shall run to and fro, and knowledge shall increase" (Daniel 12:4). As previously mentioned, another sign of the end times is a vast increase in knowledge, with developments in technology being among the greatest advances. The website Industry Tap posted an article about the "knowledge doubling curve," a term coined by architect and futurist Buckminster Fuller. Fuller "noticed that until 1900 human knowledge doubled approximately every century. By the end of World War II knowledge was doubling every 25 years." By 2013, knowledge was doubling about every thirteen months. According to IBM, before long, it will double every twelve hours![59]

We have noted how God has allowed an increase in knowledge and scientific discovery over the last century to facilitate the preaching of the gospel to the whole world through various electronic means— radio, television, cell phones, computers, tablets, and so on. However, the increase in knowledge has also led human beings to become arrogant, concluding that they are self-sufficient and do not need God—or that He does not even exist. Sometimes, the more educated people are, the more reasons they find not to believe in God. A desire for knowledge independent of the Creator is what led to the fall of mankind. The devil tempted Adam and Eve to disobey God and eat from the Tree of

59. David Russell Schilling, "Knowledge Doubling Every 12 Months, Soon to Be Every 12 Hours," Industry Tap, April 19, 2013, http://www.industrytap.com/knowledge-doubling-every-12-months-soon-to-be-every-12-hours/3950.

Knowledge of Good and Evil, saying, *"You will be like God, knowing good and evil"* (Genesis 3:5). Since that time, mankind has not been able to handle the power of knowledge without moving away from his Creator. Thus, as knowledge increases in the world, we will see people become less dependent on God.

Knowledge itself is not evil. What is evil is when we allow ourselves to be deceived about our supposed autonomy to the point of denying our Creator, who is the cornerstone of all knowledge. God's knowledge surpasses human reason. No matter to what heights of scientific achievement we may attain, our intellect is still inferior to the mind of God, which contains all the secrets of natural and supernatural life.

> **HOWEVER GREAT IT MAY BE, MANKIND'S KNOWLEDGE IS NATURAL AND LIMITED. GOD'S KNOWLEDGE IS SUPERNATURAL AND UNLIMITED.**

We must completely place our faith in God. We cannot trust mere human knowledge if we are to face the supernatural events looming over this generation. To help us in these end times, even as mankind's knowledge increases, God is releasing revealed knowledge in the church as never before. We are living in a period of revelation. These are the days when our revelation must be greater than our education.

The last book of the Bible is called *Revelation*. The Greek word translated *"revelation," apokalypsis*, means "appearing, coming, lighten, manifestation, be revealed, revelation." Seek God and receive the revelation He is imparting to the church in these last days.

THE SHORTENING OF TIME

"And unless those days were shortened, no flesh would be saved; but for the elect's sake those days will be shortened" (Matthew 24:22). Remember

that in the end times, a year will feel like a month, a month like a week, a week like a day, an hour like a minute, and a minute like a second. Although we have the same seven days in a week and the same twelve months in a year, we are experiencing an undeniable acceleration of time. The reason time has been shortened is for the sake of the remnant—because God loves His chosen ones and wants to gather them to Himself. He does not want their hope to falter and be lost. While, in one sense, time is passing by very quickly, the Lord is also holding back the end of the age because He is waiting to save those who will still believe in Him.

> But, beloved, do not forget this one thing, that with the Lord one day is as a thousand years, and a thousand years as one day. The Lord is not slack concerning His promise, as some count slackness, but is longsuffering toward us, not willing that any should perish but that all should come to repentance. (2 Peter 3:8–10)

Nevertheless, the day is coming when time will be no more. In Revelation 10, John wrote that he saw a strong angel who *"swore by Him who lives forever and ever, who created heaven and the things that are in it, the earth and the things that are in it, and the sea and the things that are in it, that there should be delay no longer"* (Revelation 10:6).

Regardless of who you are, you must admit to sensing this acceleration of time. Just remember that it is God who is doing it because He loves us. If you want to serve God, do it now. If you want to consecrate yourself and commit yourself to Him, do it now!

THE REBIRTH OF THE NATION OF ISRAEL

"Then He spoke to them a parable: 'Look at the fig tree, and all the trees. When they are already budding, you see and know for yourselves that summer is now near'" (Luke 21:29–30). Again, the rebirth of the nation of Israel is one of the greatest signs of Jesus's imminent return, both for the church and the world. Without the restoration of Israel, the prophetic promises are incomplete. God gave Israel a set time to become a nation. It was reborn during a period we can still consider to be our

generation. Therefore, one of the clearest and most indispensable signs of the coming of the Son of God has been fulfilled in our time.

This fact should serve as a warning to those countries that want to divide the land of Israel. Governments or nations that try to do so will be cursed, for the restoration of Israel as a nation is a divine act, not a human one. In its email report of November 13, 2019, Christians United for Israel (CUFI) stated that more than three hundred missiles were launched against Israel in less than a week. This occurred after Israel eliminated a terrorist leader responsible for the greatest terrorist activity, including missiles, snipers, and drones, emanating from the Gaza Strip (the Islamic Jihad of Palestine) and targeting innocent Israelis. This is just one example of the constant attack God's chosen nation has experienced. But nothing can destroy what God has done!

APOSTASY

"Now the Spirit expressly says that in latter times some will depart from the faith, giving heed to deceiving spirits and doctrines of demons" (1 Timothy 4:1). "Let no one deceive you by any means; for that Day will not come unless the falling away comes first, and the man of sin is revealed, the son of perdition" (2 Thessalonians 2:3). The Greek word for "falling away," apostasia, can also mean "defection from truth" or "forsake." To be an apostate is to disassociate oneself from, or to renounce, the faith.

The Scriptures warn us about apostasy in the last days, and tragically, we will see an increase in the number of people departing from the faith. If any generation has had apostasy at its forefront, it is ours. This should not surprise us but rather alert us to a further sign of the end times. We know we are living in the midst of increased apostasy because it is more fashionable today to be on the side of what the prevailing culture says is truth, to go along with the collective flow, rather than to stand strong and side with the truth in Christ. We are living in times when many people in the church are renouncing their faith in Jesus, the supernatural, the cross, the Holy Spirit, and the power of God because they have listened to deceiving spirits and other demonic doctrines.

When people renounce their faith in Christ and blaspheme, or speak evil, against the Holy Spirit, they commit a sin that cannot be forgiven.

Assuredly, I say to you, all sins will be forgiven the sons of men, and whatever blasphemies they may utter; but he who blasphemes against the Holy Spirit never has forgiveness, but is subject to eternal condemnation.   (Mark 3:28–29)

For it is impossible for those who were once enlightened, and have tasted the heavenly gift, and have become partakers of the Holy Spirit, and have tasted the good word of God and the powers of the age to come, if they fall away, to renew them again to repentance, since they crucify again for themselves the Son of God, and put Him to an open shame.   (Hebrews 6:4–6)

> **APOSTASY BEGINS WITHIN A PERSON WHEN THEY REJECT THE TRUTH. THEN, GOD GIVES THEM OVER TO A SPIRIT OF DECEPTION.**

PERPLEXITY

"And there will be signs in the sun, in the moon, and in the stars; and on the earth distress of nations, with perplexity, the sea and the waves roaring" (Luke 21:25). The Greek word translated *"perplexity"* means "a state of quandary." People feel perplexed when they think there is no way out of their troubles.

Dealing with a state of perplexity is a sign of the end times that we are clearly seeing firsthand. It is not just something we hear about that is happening to people in other parts of the world. Before our eyes, we see people confused and bewildered about how to remedy difficult personal and social issues. As we have discussed, events are occurring on the earth for which no one has an answer or a way out. The people of the world will not know what to do about the troubles they will experience globally and in their communities. Governments will look for solutions to environmental concerns, poverty, economic crises, and more, but they will find no answers. Neither will aid organizations or scientists. Only God has the solutions, and therefore the remnant church must be ready to receive and provide God's answers to the impossible situations we are experiencing today.

SHAKINGS

"Immediately after the tribulation of those days the sun will be darkened, and the moon will not give its light; the stars will fall from heaven, and the powers of the heavens will be shaken" (Matthew 24:29). I will not expand on this point here, since we have already studied it in detail in previous chapters. I will only remind you that God will use these times of shaking to purify the remnant bride for the appearing of His Son.

HOW TO PREPARE FOR THE END TIMES

These are not times when we should be depending on our own strength, intelligence, knowledge, or natural abilities. The only way to be prepared for what is happening and for what will come is to maintain two vital positions: (1) "watch and pray" and (2) persevere. Only in these ways will our spiritual eyes be able to see what is coming and our spirits be ready to receive the Holy Spirit's wisdom to guide us to a good end in the midst of any end-time storm.

WATCH AND PRAY

Watch and pray, lest you enter into temptation. The spirit indeed is willing, but the flesh is weak.
(Matthew 26:41)

Take heed, watch and pray; for you do not know when the time is. It is like a man going to a far country, who left his house and gave authority to his servants, and to each his work, and commanded the doorkeeper to watch. Watch therefore, for you do not know when the master of the house is coming—in the evening, at midnight, at the crowing of the rooster, or in the morning—lest, coming suddenly, he find you sleeping. And what I say to you, I say to all: Watch!

(Mark 13:33–37)

Watch therefore, and pray always that you may be counted worthy to escape all these things that will come to pass, and to stand before the Son of Man. (Luke 21:36)

Remember therefore how you have received and heard; hold fast and repent. Therefore if you will not watch, I will come upon you as a thief, and you will not know what hour I will come upon you.

(Revelation 3:3)

Throughout His ministry, Jesus repeated the admonition to "watch and pray." To watch means to be alert, awake, vigilant—all the time—so that we can pray about what we perceive in the spiritual realm. We cannot pray properly if we have a sleeping spirit. That is, if we pray, yet our spirit is not watching, our prayers will be based on our natural sight and understanding, and they will be ineffective. Only if we are watching, only if our spirit is alert, attentive, and connected to the Spirit of God, can we keep our lamps filled with oil and be ready when the bridegroom comes for His bride.

DUE TO THE OPENING OF NEW SPIRITUAL PORTALS, THE OUTPOURING OF THE SPIRIT WILL CAUSE THE SIGNS OF JESUS'S RETURN TO INTENSIFY AND INCREASE.

Remember, in these end times, new spiritual portals have been opened on the earth! There is spiritual activity taking place across the world, and if you don't progress in your spiritual knowledge and understanding, you won't be able to recognize or comprehend what is occurring. Because of the opening of these portals, time will be shortened even more, so watch and pray!

PERSEVERE

"But he who endures to the end shall be saved" (Matthew 24:13). In other words, Jesus is saying, "He who continues in their faith in Me will be saved." This verse does not align with the doctrine of "once saved, always saved." There's a reason why following such a false belief is dangerous. Jesus tells us that amid all the signs of the end times that are taking place, we cannot let ourselves be defeated or deviate from the path the Lord has marked out for us until He returns. We must persevere until the very end.

In God's mind, it does not matter where we were last year or even last week. What matters is where we are today. *"By your patience possess your souls"* (Luke 21:19). We might have been faithful for our entire lives up to this point, but if we are not continuing in God today, if we have stopped persevering, we will not "possess our souls." The day we were saved, our names were written in the Book of Life. However, the Bible says some names will be blotted out of that book. *"He who overcomes shall be clothed in white garments, and I will not blot out his name from the Book of Life; but I will confess his name before My Father and before His angels"* (Revelation 3:5). If a name can be erased, it is because it was written down in the first place; this proves that salvation is something we can lose if we do not faithfully maintain it, trusting in God to sustain us. This is a race of endurance; it's not so much how you start or even how fast you run but rather how you finish. Let's stay the course!

BE READY!

As the end times culminate, we will see more record-breaking calamities in nature and in the world economy. More violence and apostasy will take place. Everything will intensify! Natural man will try to explain these developments through science and logic, but we must understand that the signs will strengthen and become more frequent because of the spiritual movements that are signaling the end times. What is most important is for you to be ready so that you can persevere to the end.

Therefore, let us watch and pray so that we will not fall into temptation, and, above all, so that we will be alert for the coming of Christ! Let us be part of the remnant that is without *"spot or wrinkle"* (Ephesians 5:27), fully clothed (see Revelation 3:18), with our lamps continually filled with oil (see Matthew 25:1–13). Let us persevere to the end until we reach the fullness of our salvation! Christ is coming soon!

SUMMARY

- God's judgment on mankind's rebellion, sin, and evil is coming to the earth. The signs are clear.

- The most striking signs of the end times are the following:

  » Deception, which is a perversion of the truth (see Matthew 24:4–5, 11, 24)

  » False prophets, those who have a spirit of impersonation, deception, or pretense (see Matthew 24:5, 11)

  » Wars and rumors of war (see Matthew 24:6; Luke 21:9)

  » Nation rising against nation, which refers to races and ethnic groups in conflict with one another (see Matthew 24:7)

  » Famine and pestilence (see Matthew 24:7; Luke 21:11)

  » Earthquakes (see Matthew 24:7; Luke 21:25)

  » Persecution of the church (see Matthew 24:9; Luke 21:12)

  » Offenses, as a satanic strategy to remove Christians from the remnant church (see Matthew 24:10)

  » Lawlessness, or iniquity; this is the equivalent of rebellion and is a mark of the antichrist spirit (see Matthew 24:12)

  » Love growing cold, which refers to leaving one's first love for Christ due to disillusionment, hurt, bitterness, selfishness, or apathy (see Matthew 24:12)

  » The preaching of the gospel in all the world (see Matthew 24:14)

  » Fear, especially unfounded apprehensions caused by the increased presence of the dark side of the supernatural on the earth (see Luke 21:26)

  » An increase in knowledge (see Daniel 12:4)

» The shortening of time, which is due to God's love for His chosen ones, to keep their hope from faltering (see Matthew 24:22)

» The rebirth of the nation of Israel (see Luke 21:29–30)

» Apostasy (1 Timothy 4:1)

» Perplexity, or the sense that there is no way out of one's troubles (Luke 21:25)

» Shakings (see Matthew 24:29)

+ To be prepared for the end times, we must maintain two essential positions: (1) watch and pray, and (2) persevere.

SIGNS OF THE TIMES TESTIMONIES

RENNY MCLEAN'S SUPERNATURAL REVELATIONS

We know that God is calling His remnant to prepare the way for the second coming of the Lord Jesus. Among those who are called is my friend Apostle Renny McLean, who is a prophetic voice in our day. He travels the world proclaiming the coming climax of the end times with revelation, miracles, and supernatural manifestations.

Renny was born in London. His mother was of Jewish origin and his father was Jamaican. However, his mother had become a believer in Jesus Christ, and he was brought up as a Christian. While he was still young, he had an experience in which his spirit was taken up into heaven. Here he describes his encounters with God and his thoughts on the second coming.

My wife, Dr. Marina McLean, and I founded Renny McLean Ministries, whose mission is to enrich and spiritually empower the lives of all people in the three dimensions of the supernatural: faith, the anointing, and the glory of God. Both Marina and I grew up knowing the Lord. As a result, we have seen massive transformation and impact in our lives and in the lives of those around us.

My mother was a Sephardic Jew, but her parents did not pass on much of their Jewish heritage to their children. Therefore, I don't come from an Orthodox Jewish upbringing. However, my mother became a believer in Christ, and she raised me in the church. When I was fourteen, I met my grandmother on my mother's side, and she led me to understand my Jewish heritage.

My personal experiences in learning God's ways began when I was very young. In April 1972, when I was seven, I had a supernatural encounter with God that placed my faith in a higher dimension. Since then, I have seen the Lord many times. He revealed Himself to me in a supernatural way, opening my eyes to the Bible as His living Word. I had an encounter with the Author of Scripture! Throughout my life, the Lord has visited me either through the appearances of angels or of Jesus Himself. God commissioned me to raise people up in His power and glory and teach them to move in the power of the Spirit.

While I was reading the Old Testament, God gave me a revelation of the spiritual meaning of the feasts of the Lord. Much of the church believes a traditional teaching about eschatology that is erroneous. Because the church has replaced the feasts of the Lord with the teaching of dispensationalism, most Christians do not know the relationship between the feasts and the signs of the times. This is the missing component in much of denominational theology.

My revelation of the second coming of Christ has affected my view of the church, the world, and Israel. It has led me to understand the role of the church in the end times and to see everything with spiritual eyes, to always be in a state of urgency and readiness. Because the second coming is near, the true state of the church and of individual believers is being exposed, revealing both the apostate church and the remnant bride. Each of these groups can be identified by the measure of their knowledge of God. The apostate church has conformed to the spirit of this age and reduced its effectiveness in society, while the remnant has a passion for the Lord and an unshakable faith that remains firm.

Among the signs of the end times, miracles will become more prophetic in nature and healings will multiply. I believe we will see miracles on a national level, similar to those that were manifested through Moses when he went before Pharaoh in Egypt. Those miracles will occur if the church speaks the truth with power. *Maranatha*! Christ is coming!

SID ROTH'S RADICAL ENCOUNTER WITH THE MESSIAH

Sid Roth was born in the United States to a Jewish family. As a young man, he began to pursue his dream of becoming a millionaire and worked for one of the world's largest brokerage firms. However, Sid had an encounter with God that changed him completely, and he became a believer in Jesus as the Messiah. Sid continues to grow in the vision that God has given him. He hosts the television show *It's Supernatural!* in order to share the good news of the Messiah with the world, "*for the Jew first and also for the Greek*" (Romans 1:16).[60]

My name is Sid Roth, and I am a citizen of both Israel and the United States. As a child, I attended synagogue and celebrated my bar mitzvah. When I reached adulthood, I was proud to be Jewish but bored with religion. To be honest, my god was money. I wanted to be a millionaire by age thirty. By the time I was twenty-nine, I had graduated from college, gotten married, had a daughter, and worked as an account executive for Merrill Lynch, but I considered myself a failure because I was not yet a millionaire.

Deep down, I felt a longing. There had to be something more to life...but I couldn't find it in religion. I believed in a God who was so far away that He had become irrelevant. So, I left my

---

60. To learn more about how Jews and others are being reached for Christ through Sid's ministry, visit https://sidroth.org/about/about-ministry/.

wife, my daughter, and my job and went in search of that "something else." After a year, I still had not found the answer, so I took a meditation course, where I was taught to lower my brain waves and, in that passive, hypnotic state, to invite a "counselor" into my head who would answer all my questions.

About that time, I wanted to open my own investment business. Almost immediately, an entrepreneur offered me an office, a secretary, and a free phone. When I accepted his offer, he asked me, "Sid, do you know that your own Jewish Bible condemns any involvement in the occult?" He showed me Deuteronomy 18:10–12 in the Torah and told me that the "counselor" I was consulting was not from God. I decided to find out if the Bible was really the Word of God. As I began to read the Scriptures, I had the shock of my life. My "counselor" began to curse me. Things got worse, and I went into astral projection. This is where your spirit temporarily leaves your body. In that state, death seemed to be my only way out.

The businessman who had given me the free office for my investment company was a Christian. He told me that Jesus was the Messiah, and He would help me in times of crisis. He gave me a little book that explained my need, as a Jew, for the Messiah. It said that before the Messiah came, we Jews had our sins covered on Yom Kippur (the Day of Atonement) through the sacrifice of an animal in the temple. Today, we have no temple for animal sacrifices. But by believing in the death and resurrection of the Messiah, our sins would be forgiven, and we would regain our ability to experientially know God.

The little book invited people to pray a prayer for salvation, which I did. At the time, nothing appeared to happen, and I thought it didn't "work." But God had heard me and changed my spiritual DNA. Several days later, on the worst night of my life, I prayed a two-word prayer: "Jesus, help!" I went to sleep not wanting to wake up again. But the next morning, I immediately knew that something had changed. The evil inside me was gone, and I was no longer afraid. I felt surrounded by liquid love, a love so pure! It was the tangible presence of God. I had never felt such peace! And I was convinced that Jesus was my Messiah.

Then, I heard the voice of God telling me to go home. My wife had become an agnostic in college, but when I showed her the predictions about Israel written in the Scriptures thousands of years ago, she believed. Soon afterward, she received Jesus. My mother thought I was just going through another phase that would pass, but my father became angry and accused me of reading a Christian Bible, as if it were any different from the Jewish one.

The entire history of the Jewish people, past, present, and future, is in the Bible, along with hundreds of predictions that have already been accurately fulfilled. For example, David described the death of the Messiah hundreds of years before the first recorded crucifixion. His exact words were fulfilled a thousand years later when Jesus was crucified. Furthermore, the scientific dating of the Dead Sea Scrolls in Israel proves that no one incorporated the Bible's predictions after the events occurred.

Against all logic and possibility, for thousands of years, God has preserved the Jews as a different and marked people. God gave a great sign, greater than the dry crossing of the Red Sea. That sign was the nation of Israel being formed in one day, just as Isaiah had predicted. The prophet Amos said that when the Lord returned, we would rebuild the desolate cities. Tel Aviv is as modern and cosmopolitan as any advanced city in the world. How did Isaiah know, twenty-seven hundred years ago, that Israel would develop technology that would bring groundwater to the surface to irrigate the vegetation of a barren desert? Today, the problems of Jerusalem and the small nation of Israel are in the world news all the time. And God is still working out His purposes for Israel and the world.

In the end, my father and mother accepted Jesus as their Messiah and Lord. I am so grateful! Today, every member of my immediate family believes in Jesus. Every day, I experience God's presence, and I have seen thousands of miracles as a result of praying in Jesus's name. God wants to place His Spirit within us and give us new hearts filled with His love. Some people, like me, will have a radical encounter with Him as they come to believe in the Messiah. Others will quietly accept His forgiveness by faith. To know God is everything. To have "everything" yet not know God is nothing. If you don't know Him before you die, you won't know Him after you die. The time to know God and receive Jesus is now!

CHAPTER 6

HOW TO IDENTIFY THE REMNANT BRIDE

In chapter 5, we reviewed descriptions of end-times signs and of Jesus's return from various biblical passages, including Matthew 24. In this chapter, we move on to Matthew 25, where Jesus delineated the qualities of His remnant bride. By taking a close look at the parable of the ten virgins, we can identify who will be part of the remnant in these last days.

To understand this parable, it is necessary to have some background on ancient Hebrew culture and the history of Israel's relationship with the Lord. After liberating the Israelites from oppression in Egypt and making a covenant with them on Mount Sinai, God referred to Himself as the Israelites' husband. (See Jeremiah 31:32.) Other Old Testament passages use similar marriage imagery. (See, for example, Isaiah 54:5–6; Jeremiah 3:1, 8, 14.)

In the New Testament, we read about the betrothal between Christ and the church. This marriage has not yet taken place but will occur in the fullness of the times. Paul wrote, *"For this reason a man shall leave his father and mother and be joined to his wife, and the two shall become one flesh.' This is a great mystery, but I speak concerning Christ and the church"* (Ephesians 5:31–32).

In Hebrew culture, when a woman was to be married, her groom had to give her nine gifts. These gifts represented the nine gifts of the Holy Spirit, which are bestowed on the church. (See 1 Corinthians 12:4, 7–10.) If spiritual gifts are not active in our lives, we lack the power of the Holy Spirit that Jesus grants to His bride.

In addition, it was common for the father of the family to select a bride for his son, and then he would present the chosen woman to his son to marry. In the Old Testament, we see an example of this practice where Abraham entrusted his servant with a vital task: *"You shall go to my country and to my family, and take a wife for my son Isaac"* (Genesis 24:4). The servant prayed for guidance, and the Lord led him straight to Rebekah, who became Isaac's bride. (See verses 5–66.)

The New Testament explains that God the Father gives the church (the bride) to His Son Jesus (the Bridegroom King). In other words, the Father is the One who chooses the bride. Jesus recognizes only those whom the Father presents to Him. He said, *"No one can come to Me unless the Father who sent Me draws him; and I will raise him up at the last day"* (John 6:44). Thus, if someone approaches Jesus whom the Father has not sent, He will not know them. This is one of the reasons why, as we will shortly see in the parable of the wise and foolish virgins, Jesus said to the five foolish virgins, *"I do not know you"* (Matthew 25:12).

Just as Abraham sent his servant to choose a wife for his son, the heavenly Father sends the Holy Spirit to choose the bride of Christ. The Holy Spirit will choose for Jesus those who have been processed to be the remnant. This is why we must have a close relationship with the Holy Spirit and be filled with His power to even be considered as a candidate for the bride of Christ.

At most weddings, invited guests come to witness the ceremony. The guests must arrive before the wedding begins if they are to fully participate in the event. In the context of Jesus's forthcoming marriage to the church, who are the guests? They are the believers who lived before the church age, like David and Abraham, whose faith *"was accounted to him for righteousness"* (Romans 4:22). These believers are now in heaven, waiting for the bride. (See, for example, Hebrews 12:1–2.) The Groom is at the altar, also awaiting the bride. Jesus has been waiting for a long time. Will you be among those who are His bride?

JESUS RECOGNIZES AS THE BRIDE ONLY THOSE WHOM THE FATHER PRESENTS TO HIM.

In Ephesians 4, Paul gives us instructions for becoming mature believers in Jesus. Then, in chapter 5, he speaks of the mature church, or what I like to call "the remnant." As the remnant grows in love and faith, being transformed into the bride of Christ, it will also develop purer worship. It will worship *"in spirit and truth"* (John 4:23–24). Much of the church today has replaced genuine worship with mere entertainment. Christians are deceived, not recognizing the difference between the two. Rather than offering total devotion to God, they feed their own emotions and fleshly appetites. George Barna wrote a book entitled *The Seven Faith Tribes* based on his research into seven diverse faith groups in the United States. One of those "tribes" is labeled "casual Christians," which represent 66 percent of the adult population. Another tribe, called "captive Christians" or committed Christians, represents only 16 percent.[61] This minority may be recognized as the remnant.

---

61. "Casual Christians and the Future of America," Barna Group, May 25, 2009, https://www.barna.com/research/casual-christians-and-the-future-of-america/.

If you do not engage in genuine worship, you are not part of the bride of Christ. In the end times, the remnant will worship by singing songs about the names of God, about Christ's finished work on the cross, and about God's glory.

THE PARABLE OF THE WISE AND FOOLISH VIRGINS

Let's look now at Jesus's parable of the wise and foolish virgins. No biblical parable depicts the condition of today's church better than this one!

> *Then the kingdom of heaven shall be likened to ten virgins who took their lamps and went out to meet the bridegroom. Now five of them were wise, and five were foolish. Those who were foolish took their lamps and took no oil with them, but the wise took oil in their vessels with their lamps.* (Matthew 25:1–4)

First, let us define some terms so that we can better understand the revelation of this parable. To begin, the word *parable* is defined as a "narrative of an imaginary event from which, by comparison or similarity, an important truth or moral teaching is deduced."[62] The parable of the wise and foolish virgins is an earthly story with a heavenly meaning.

This parable features several symbolic characters: five wise virgins, five foolish virgins, and the bridegroom. A virgin is a man or woman who has never been sexually intimate. Jesus used this analogy to symbolize the pure nature of the true church. The groom represents the ascended Jesus, who returns at the rapture to carry away His bride to heaven. The parable also mentions two significant items: lamps and oil. The lamps signify God's Word (see, for example, Psalm 119:105), and the oil represents the power of the Holy Spirit to light our way, which is available to us through a life of prayer and intimacy with God.

Since all ten virgins were carrying lamps, this means they were walking in the Word of God. However, five of them carried extra oil to

---

62. English translation of the definition of the Spanish word *parabola*, Real Academia Española, https://dle.rae.es/?w=par%C3%A1bola.

refill their lamps when the need arose. This means that the five foolish ones began well; they were virgins and had their lamps. But they acted foolishly by not bringing reserve oil. It is useless to carry lamps if we do not have oil with which to light them. Jesus warns us against such foolishness. It is not enough to have had a relationship with the Lord in the past or to know His Word if we do not also have the revelation of the Holy Spirit and live according to the Word daily. Today, many churches flat-out reject the ministry of the Holy Spirit!

In addition to the power of the Holy Spirit, the oil represents the person of the Spirit. It signifies the entire spiritual realm of God, including supernatural power, the anointing, the gifts of the Spirit, and the fruit of the Spirit. Let me reemphasize that we cannot take part in the rapture while rejecting the person of the Holy Spirit, denying His power, and lacking His gifts and fruit.

The rest of the parable reads as follows:

> But while the bridegroom was delayed, [the ten virgins] all slumbered and slept. And at midnight a cry was heard: "Behold, the bridegroom is coming; go out to meet him!" Then all those virgins arose and trimmed their lamps. And the foolish said to the wise, "Give us some of your oil, for our lamps are going out." But the wise answered, saying, "No, lest there should not be enough for us and you; but go rather to those who sell, and buy for yourselves." And while they went to buy, the bridegroom came, and those who were ready went in with him to the wedding; and the door was shut. Afterward the other virgins came also, saying, "Lord, Lord, open to us!" But he answered and said, "Assuredly, I say to you, I do not know you." Watch therefore, for you know neither the day nor the hour in which the Son of Man is coming.   (Matthew 25:5–13)

THE NECESSITY OF HAVING OIL IN OUR LAMPS

Because the bridegroom was delayed, the ten virgins were overcome with weariness and they fell asleep. The bridegroom didn't arrive at an hour they expected but rather at midnight. Hearing the announcement that he had come, which is often referred to as the "midnight cry" in its prophetic context, they all woke up, but only five of them had enough oil for their lamps to go and meet the bridegroom.

Only if a lamp has a source of power can it be lit, illuminating its surroundings. If we do not have the Holy Spirit as our spiritual power source, we will not have the necessary light to see in these dark times. Again, we can only acquire the presence of the Spirit through a continuous and intimate relationship with Him. We cannot depend on others to obtain this relationship for us.

In the parable, the foolish virgins had to go out and buy more oil. However, upon their return, they were disheartened to learn that the bridegroom had already come and entered the wedding feast with the guests who were ready for him—including the five wise virgins—and that the door had been shut. Jesus concluded the parable with the moral to the story: *"Watch therefore, for you know neither the day nor the hour in which the Son of Man is coming"* (Matthew 25:13). In the original Greek, the verb is in the imperative mood, forming the command *"Watch."*

Unfortunately, the spirit of this age has brought a deep sleep upon the church, keeping it from watching for the Bridegroom. Many Christians are living in darkness because they lack oil for their lamps. People are burned out and exhausted because they are preoccupied with the cares of life. They are primarily focused on transient concerns that do not have eternal significance.

> *But take heed to yourselves, lest your hearts be weighed down with carousing, drunkenness, and cares of this life, and that Day come on you unexpectedly. For it will come as a snare on all those who dwell on the face of the whole earth. Watch therefore, and pray always that you may be counted worthy to escape all these things that will come to pass, and to stand before the Son of Man.* (Luke 21:34–36)

> *Therefore He says: "Awake, you who sleep, arise from the dead, and Christ will give you light."* (Ephesians 5:14)

"Watching" is synonymous with being wise. Like the five wise virgins who carried reserve oil for their lamps, we need to exercise wisdom by seeking to be filled with the Holy Spirit at all times. Remember, we cannot continue walking with the faith, the anointing, or the infilling of the Spirit that we had last week, much less last year. With the Spirit, it's all about what happens *now*. Is your relationship with God current? Does your lamp have oil, and are you continually replenishing that oil?

> **IF WE DO NOT HAVE THE HOLY SPIRIT AS OUR SPIRITUAL POWER SOURCE, WE WILL NOT HAVE THE NECESSARY LIGHT TO SEE IN THESE DARK TIMES.**

THE MISSING ELEMENT

Let's go even deeper into the meaning of this parable. Five virgins were wise and five were foolish, but they were all virgins. Their virginity represents believing in Christ, living a holy life, regularly fellowshipping with other believers, meeting the needs of people, and so forth. All ten virgins had these characteristics. However, the five foolish virgins represent those who believe in Jesus but have in some way rejected the person or work of the Holy Spirit. The parable reveals a mystery that I have tried to communicate in various ways throughout this book: not all Christians are part of the bride of Christ who will be taken when He appears.

Thus, the Lord used this parable to symbolize the state of the church at His return. It is a clear warning that we can be good people yet still not be right with God and, therefore, not be ready for Jesus's coming. We can be believers and go to church but still not be prepared as the bride to meet the Bridegroom. I know good Christian people who do not believe in the Holy Spirit or His power. It grieves me to know they will not go with Christ in the rapture. Only a portion of the church will be taken. It is tragic that this generation of believers is spiritually asleep. Because they don't know that the time of Jesus's appearing is drawing near, they have neglected to make preparations to meet Him.

Once more, the major deficiency in the five foolish virgins was their shortage of oil. The shortage represents a lack of intimacy with God, ability to hear His voice, spirituality, anointing, and power. Do we not see the same deficiency in much of Christianity today? A Pew Research Center article reported that 55 percent of Americans say they pray daily.[63] I wonder, though, how many people in this percentage have an intimate relationship with God beyond making requests and offering occasional thanks. According to Barna Group, which has been tracking people's prayer habits since 1993, 69 percent of Americans reported praying at least once a week. This number declined from about 83 percent over the decade of 2011 to 2020.[64] In a report by *U.S. News* and Beliefnet, only about 42 percent of Christians surveyed said that the *most* important purpose of prayer is to have intimacy with God.[65] To me, that minority percentage looks very much like a remnant.

Without the Holy Spirit, the church is dry and dead. It has no real purpose or power. Many believers may be using their gifts, including spiritual gifts, but they are only exercising them mechanically. It is possible for a church to look and sound spiritual but completely lack God's presence. In the parable, when the bridegroom comes, the decisive factor for the virgins regarding whether they can enter the marriage feast is not the lamps they are carrying but rather what is—or isn't—inside them. If we do not have the power of the Holy Spirit within us, we will only have a *"form of godliness"* (2 Timothy 3:5), making us simply an institution of religious people, a human organization, rather than the true house of

63. Michael Lipka, "5 Facts About Prayer," Pew Research Center, Washington, D.C., May 4, 2016, https://www.pewresearch.org/fact-tank/2016/05/04/5-facts-about-prayer/.
64. "Signs of Decline & Hope Among Key Metrics of Faith," Barna Group, March 4, 2020, https://www.barna.com/research/changing-state-of-the-church/.
65. "U.S. News & Beliefnet Prayer Survey Results," Beliefnet, December 2004, https://www.beliefnet.com/faiths/faith-tools/meditation/2004/12/u-s-news-beliefnet-prayer-survey-results.aspx.

God. We need the Holy Spirit's fire to light our lamps so that we may remain close to God and so that His Word may burn within us and enlighten our understanding.

WITHOUT THE HOLY SPIRIT, ALL CHURCH ACTIVITY IS MECHANICAL AND EMPTY OF GOD.

The five foolish virgins were inactive when they should have been diligent to make sure they had enough oil. Similarly, the church today is spiritually lukewarm, passive, indifferent, uncommitted, insensitive, dry, blind, asleep, and even spiritually dead. One result is that due to their weak spiritual condition, Christians often seek to be inoffensive and nonconfrontational about the gospel message, so they water down the good news, making it powerless to change people's lives.

In the book of Revelation, Jesus admonished seven different churches, several of which exhibited some of the above characteristics, demonstrating their tenuous spiritual states. For example, the Lord rebuked the church at Ephesus for neglecting their foremost spiritual priority: "*Nevertheless I have this against you, that you have left your first love. Remember therefore from where you have fallen; repent and do the first works*" (Revelation 2:4–5). If the five foolish virgins had been committed to meeting the bridegroom and attending the wedding, they would have made sure they had all the supplies they needed beforehand. The majority of the church today is failing to prepare for Jesus's return because it has lost its love for Him and is no longer committed to His purposes.

Jesus warned the church in Sardis that they were spiritually asleep: "*I know your works, that you have a name that you are alive, but you are dead. Be watchful, and strengthen the things which remain, that are ready to die*" (Revelation 3:1–2). Again, the foolish virgins were sleeping when they should have been looking for oil to trim their lamps so they could meet the bridegroom. Consequently, they missed his arrival. Likewise, the contemporary church is in a deep sleep and thus neglecting to watch for the Bridegroom. It is in danger of missing out when the Lord appears!

Jesus's words to the church in Laodicea were especially strong. The state of this church was just as dire as that of the others, and it had all the negative characteristics we see in the church today:

> *These things says the Amen, the Faithful and True Witness, the Beginning of the creation of God: "I know your works, that you are neither cold nor hot. I could wish you were cold or hot. So then, because you are lukewarm, and neither cold nor hot, I will vomit you out of My mouth. Because you say, 'I am rich, have become wealthy, and have need of nothing'—and do not know that you are wretched, miserable, poor, blind, and naked."* (Revelation 3:14–17)

Because I carry the fear of God in my heart, I pray to the Father every day that my oil will never run out and my lamp will never go out. Because I know I must continually stay in close fellowship with the Lord, I have made prayer a way of life. In fact, my whole ministry depends on my prayer life as I rely entirely on God. Just as the Scriptures teach us, I pray for God's people and for the governing authorities in my own country and other countries of the world. Recently, I took part in a meeting with a group of the most influential pastors in America and the president of the United States, Donald Trump. This event was significant because it was the first time a president had gone to evangelical pastors for advice and wisdom, publicly receiving their prayers. I believe this was the president's way of demonstrating a fear of God and asking for fresh oil for his lamp. God gave me the opportunity to pray for him, and I asked the Lord to fill Him with the Holy Spirit, strengthen him, and give him wisdom to do His will.

Now, more than ever, we must pray for our governmental leaders. Remember, there is no rational way out of the crises we are facing. It will take God's wisdom to overcome them. I encourage you to pray for all those in authority. (See 1 Timothy 2:1–2.)

THE REMNANT BRIDE

How, then, can we identify the remnant bride? It is the portion of the church that fears the Lord and has a close relationship with Him. It is awake, alert, obedient, watching, and praying. It is filled with the Spirit, with God's presence, and with heavenly glory and power. It is committed, holy, passionate, and strong. The remnant lives righteously and worships God in Spirit and truth. It is a mature, spiritual church that is intimate with the Spirit of God.

God's remnant bride knows that Jesus's return is near. Therefore, the remnant prepares the way for His arrival, preaching the gospel with a sense of urgency and manifesting miracles, signs, and wonders. Every time we teach others about the second coming, we draw closer to His return! We have noted that many people do not believe in the return of the Lord because they are spiritually asleep, busy with the cares of life, and, most important, lack a reverence for God in their hearts. Are you part of the sleeping church or part of the remnant?

Voice of the Martyrs reports on believers who, as members of the remnant, are paving the way for the second coming in the face of obstacles from their families and nations and despite the contrary beliefs of their societies. A Fulani[66] teenager named Mohammed was disowned by his family for going to church. He lived in an unfinished apartment building for six years while completing school. When he was eighteen, he attempted to return home but was still rejected. With God's help, he entered a Bible school, but even there, he experienced prejudice from Christians because of his Fulani background. "If it wasn't for the love I have for Jesus, I would never have stayed a Christian," he said. Mohammed has persevered because he is committed to the Lord and will never turn away from Him.[67]

Hafiz is the son of a Fulani herdsman and a voodoo herbalist. He was in line to take over the family business from his father, who had four

---

66. An ethnic group in Africa.
67. "Rejected by His Family but Found in Christ," Voice of the Martyrs, June 25, 2019, https://vom.com.au/rejected-by-his-family-but-found-in-christ/.

wives and thirty-nine children. Hafiz came from a Muslim community that persecuted Christians in their town, killing hundreds of them. He started reading the Bible to become familiar with it so he could use the information to convert people to Islam. Instead, he was drawn to Jesus and became a Christian! When he shared his new faith with his family, his father became angry and took him to the police station, where he was locked in a cell for two years and repeatedly urged to return to Islam. When Hafiz was finally released, he fled to the safety of Youth With A Mission (YWAM). Yet he plans to return to the Fulani people, saying, "I know they are still in darkness and I want to bring them out of that through God."[68]

A woman in Malaysia named Nisa was born into a Muslim family, but after marrying a Christian and meeting his family, she had an encounter with Jesus. Her husband's brother was a pastor, and he spoke to her about the Lord. Initially, she wasn't interested, but one day, she let her brother-in-law pray for her. "Once he laid hands on me and prayed," she says, "I felt cold as ice and like something changed my heart and I just broke down and wept and wept." After Nisa became a Christian, her parents became believers, too, but many of her other family members became hostile toward her. She continues to hold on to her faith in Christ despite poverty and persecution—all because someone prayed for her.[69]

At my church, King Jesus Ministry, we know that Christ is coming soon, and we actively seek to remain part of the remnant bride. We go out to the streets to evangelize and hold miracle crusades all over the world, manifesting miracles, signs, and wonders through the power of the Holy Spirit. We travel to areas where the gospel has not yet been preached and bring revival to places where being a Christian is illegal. We go to spheres of human power, such as high levels of government and business, to reach people who would never come near a church. We have an active

---

68. "Former Fulani Herdsman Called to Evangelise," Voice of the Martyrs, June 25, 2019, https://vom.com.au/former-fulani-herdsman-called-to-evangelise/.
69. "Finding Christ in Malaysia," Voice of the Martyrs, April 28, 2019, https://vom.com.au/finding-christ-in-malaysia/.

intercession team that is watching and praying twenty-four hours a day with their eyes on the spiritual world. We want to prepare the way for Jesus's return and be ready to go with Him at His appearance!

THE MIDNIGHT CRY

"And at midnight a cry was heard: 'Behold, the bridegroom is coming; go out to meet him!'" (Matthew 25:6). This part of the parable depicts the end-time cry of the Bridegroom, Jesus, to His bride, the remnant. It is a call to those who are watching and praying, ready to meet Jesus in the clouds. It is a call to holiness, consecration, and separation for Him. The midnight cry signifies the turning point between night and day, and therefore it represents change. The Holy Spirit is raising a cry of holiness for us to turn away from the world and dedicate ourselves to living a righteous life, separated from the world, fleshly desires, and anything else that would distract us from our purpose in God.

A survey conducted by the Barna Group gives us an idea of the state of the church in the United States in terms of holiness. Among adult born-again Christians, 76 percent said it is possible to become holy, but only 55 percent said they knew a person they would describe as holy. Only 29 percent considered themselves to be holy. American adults most likely to say they know a holy or sanctified person defined holiness as "possessing a positive attitude toward God and life." Those least likely to identify someone they know as holy defined holiness as a "spiritual condition."[70]

> **HOLINESS MEANS BEING CONTINUOUSLY SET APART FOR GOD AND FOR A PURPOSE, SEPARATED FROM THE SPIRIT OF THE WORLD. HOLINESS IS THE MARK OF THE REMNANT BRIDE.**

---

70. "The Concept of Holiness Baffles Most Americans," Barna Group, February 20, 2006, https://www.barna.com/research/the-concept-of-holiness-baffles-most-americans/.

The world does not want Christians to hold godly values and standards. However, we are called to be like Christ in our motivations and lifestyle. A line must be drawn between the remnant and the rest. *"I beseech you therefore, brethren, by the mercies of God, that you present your bodies a living sacrifice, holy, acceptable to God, which is your reasonable service. And do not be conformed to this world, but be transformed by the renewing of your mind"* (Romans 12:1–2).

"I DO NOT KNOW YOU"

Let's review what happened to the foolish virgins after the midnight cry:

> *Then all those virgins arose and trimmed their lamps. And the foolish said to the wise, "Give us some of your oil, for our lamps are going out." But the wise answered, saying, "No, lest there should not be enough for us and you; but go rather to those who sell, and buy for yourselves." And while they went to buy, the bridegroom came, and those who were ready went in with him to the wedding; and the door was shut. Afterward the other virgins came also, saying, "Lord, Lord, open to us!" But he answered and said, "Assuredly, I say to you, **I do not know you.**"* (Matthew 25:7–12)

The Hebrew word translated *"know"* in verse 12 refers to having an intimate relationship with someone; it means knowing a person not just by sight but also deeply. We have seen that the five foolish virgins represent Christians who have not had a deep relationship with God. Always keep in mind that we might attend church, dance, pray, and give offerings but still not be intimate with God. Many believers have never known such closeness with the Lord. They have never truly walked with Him or heard His voice. God's Word is not alive in them. They may know the Lord from afar, but He does not know them. We must truly understand the reality that not every believer is included in the bride of Christ.

At the end of the parable, the door to the wedding celebration is closed and the foolish virgins arrive too late to enter in! If Jesus does not know us on earth, He won't take us to be with Him in heaven. Just as the door to the ark was shut during the worldwide flood, keeping Noah and his family safe inside but leaving everyone else on earth to face judgment (see Genesis 7), so the doors to heaven will be shut after the rapture, protecting the remnant but leaving the rest of the world to experience the judgment of the tribulation.

"For then there will be great tribulation, such as has not been since the beginning of the world until this time, no, nor ever shall be" (Matthew 24:21). The world will go mad due to the judgment God will unleash. There will be judgment after judgment on the earth.

> *By these three plagues a third of mankind was killed—by the fire and the smoke and the brimstone which came out of their mouths....*
> *But the rest of mankind, who were not killed by these plagues, did not repent of the works of their hands, that they should not worship demons, and idols of gold, silver, brass, stone, and wood, which can neither see nor hear nor walk. And they did not repent of their murders or their sorceries or their sexual immorality or their thefts.*
> (Revelation 9:18, 20–21)

When the bride is removed from the earth, the Holy Spirit will also be removed as a supernatural influence and restraint against evil in the world. *"For the mystery of lawlessness is already at work; only He who now restrains will do so until He is taken out of the way"* (2 Thessalonians 2:7). However, the believers who are not ready for Jesus's appearing and are left behind will still have the Holy Spirit living within them and thus have access to heaven. They will have the ability to reject the mark of the beast and be witnesses for Christ, even though it will likely cost them their lives. Those Christians who reject Christ at this time will be lost.

It is vital to understand that it is not enough to be a Christian, and it is not even enough to know how to manifest God's power on earth. If we do not have a genuine, constant, and intimate relationship with God, we will be left on earth at the rapture. Jesus tells us:

Not everyone who says to Me, "Lord, Lord," shall enter the kingdom of heaven, but he who does the will of My Father in heaven. Many will say to Me in that day, "Lord, Lord, have we not prophesied in Your name, cast out demons in Your name, and done many wonders in Your name?" And then I will declare to them, "I never knew you; depart from Me, you who practice lawlessness!"

(Matthew 7:21–23)

Many people are able to perform miracles while they are in a spiritual atmosphere where God's presence manifests, or while they are in association with others who are operating in a spiritual atmosphere, or when they have the spiritual gift of miracles, or even when they apply spiritual principles relating to miracles. However, they may still lack devotion to God and intimacy with the Holy Spirit. There are other people who perform miracles through demonic powers rather than God's power. Whenever we perform signs and wonders, we must make sure we do so from a place of intimacy with God or these miracles will have no eternal significance for us. The person receiving the blessing will benefit if God is doing the work, but the miracle will not enhance our standing with the Lord. Thus, it is not solely a question of our believing, doing miracles, prophesying, or casting out demons but of doing all such acts from a close relationship with God.

MIRACLES, SIGNS, AND WONDERS HAVE NO ETERNAL SIGNIFICANCE FOR THE INDIVIDUAL PERFORMING THEM IF THAT PERSON DOES NOT HAVE A LIFE OF INTIMACY WITH GOD TO BACK THEM UP.

HOW TO QUALIFY AS THE REMNANT BRIDE

I want to conclude this chapter by reviewing three fundamental ways by which we can achieve an intimate relationship with the Lord, be known by Him, and be accepted in the hour of His coming. While we have discussed these areas in previous chapters, we must never neglect them.

ALLOW YOURSELF TO BE PROCESSED

I will bring the one-third through the fire, will refine them as silver is refined, and test them as gold is tested. They will call on My name, and I will answer them. I will say, "This is My people"; and each one will say, "The LORD is my God."   (Zechariah 13:9)

Every Christian who belongs to the remnant must be processed so that their heart will be in the right place and they will maintain a close relationship with the Lord. Remember that the main purpose of processing is to enable us to grow spiritually and mature. After intimacy with God, spiritual maturity is the main qualification for being part of the remnant bride. *"And he said to me, 'Do not seal the words of the prophecy of this book, for the time is at hand. He who is unjust, let him be unjust still; he who is filthy, let him be filthy still; he who is righteous, let him be righteous still; he who is holy, let him be holy still'"* (Revelation 22:10–11). When people fail to address their sins and weaknesses, they become worse—more unjust, unclean, and depraved. This is why we cannot stagnate in our spiritual growth. We must move toward maturity, aligned with the virtues of Christ's character. (See, for example, Ephesians 4:13.)

These are perilous times. To rebel against God as He is processing us for maturity may cost us His judgment, and *"it is a fearful thing to fall into the hands of the living God"* (Hebrews 10:31). In this season, the church needs to undergo a transition if it is to become the remnant bride. The body of Christ must grow to full maturity. Matters around us will not change unless we are transformed. This will require us to submit to God as He refines us and to stand firm, knowing that we will come out of this process purer and closer to the Lord.

Everything that is not processed will die because where there is no processing, there is no transformation. If we are not transformed, we will repeat the same negative cycles that keep us spiritually immature, asleep, and unable to discern that the Lord is coming soon. Today, make sure that you are part of the remnant bride! Don't wait until Jesus returns to find out because then it will be too late.

BE CONTINUOUSLY FILLED WITH THE HOLY SPIRIT

The power of the Holy Spirit is linked to Christ's appearing. Not only is the manifestation of God's power a sign of Jesus's return, but the work of the Spirit within believers is an indispensable part of the preparation of the bride. When Christ comes, we must be able to connect with Him through the Holy Spirit's power. This is why we need to be continuously filled with the Spirit.

If there is no living, spiritual power within us with which to connect to Jesus, we will not go with Him in the rapture. As stated earlier, we might be able to do miracles or be blessed by association with someone who manifests the Spirit's power, but we will not be able to take part in the marriage of the Bridegroom by mere association. We need our own personal relationship with God and our own fire of the Holy Spirit to light our lamp and connect us with Christ, the Anointed One. Jesus will return for a church that is full of power and glory!

> *Husbands, love your wives, just as Christ also loved the church and gave Himself for her, that He might sanctify and cleanse her with the washing of water by the word, that He might present her to Himself a glorious church, not having spot or wrinkle or any such thing, but that she should be holy and without blemish.* (Ephesians 5:25–27)

It is not enough to have been filled with the Holy Spirit once, perhaps long ago. Yesterday's filling is not sufficient for today, let alone sufficient to connect with Christ at His coming. It is necessary for us to be continuously filled as we renew our relationship with God and His Spirit every day.

WATCH AND PRAY

In the previous chapter, we looked at several passages in which Jesus exhorted His followers to "watch and pray." And we have seen that Jesus gave the same vital command as a concluding statement in the parable of the wise and foolish virgins:

Watch therefore, for you know neither the day nor the hour in which the Son of Man is coming. (Matthew 25:13)

Watching and praying is essential for being established as the bride of Christ as well as for helping to usher in Jesus's coming. Let's review what it means to "watch." It means to make sure we are vigilantly connecting with the Holy Spirit, praying, being sanctified, and turning away from evil. To be watchful requires being supernaturally awake and alert to what is happening in the spiritual realm. It involves remaining in a state of readiness or preparation.

IF YOU DO NOT KEEP A VIGILANT SPIRIT, YOU WILL MISS THE RAPTURE.

"Watch therefore, and pray always that you may be counted worthy to escape all these things that will come to pass, and to stand before the Son of Man" (Luke 21:36). We stay watchful through prayer. In fact, as we discussed previously, we are to pray about what the Spirit reveals to us as we watch over our lives and the events in the world. Vigilance, then, is related to prayer. When we are watching, nothing can take us totally by surprise because watching keeps us prepared. Watching allows us to see in advance what God is planning to do and what will happen on the earth. When we are uncertain about the future, the only way to discern how to respond is to watch and pray. How often do you engage in this type of watching and praying?

The Lord will appear for those who are waiting for Him. If you have no real expectation that Jesus will return, you will not be ready for His coming. Do you understand that if you are not preparing yourself, you will be left behind on earth and have to go through the great tribulation and all the judgments? The rapture is only for the remnant that is filled with the presence and power of the Holy Spirit. If you are left on earth, the Holy Spirit will still live within you because you are a Christian. However, the Spirit will no longer be a restraining presence in the world. The tribulation will be a time of tremendous pressure and calamity in which it will be extremely difficult to remain faithful to the Lord.

DAYS OF TRANSITION

Do you have all the qualities of the remnant bride? Have you allowed God to process you in your difficulties and in the crises afflicting the world? Are you continuously being filled with the Holy Spirit? Are you constantly watching and praying? You must be able to answer yes to these questions *today*. Tomorrow will be too late!

As the coming of Christ draws nearer, we are living in days of transition. We need to mature as Christians so that His appearance does not find us unaware and unprepared. We must not run out of oil in our lamps. We have to learn to depend on the Holy Spirit so that we can understand the spiritual season we are going through and recognize how much of the Spirit's oil we actually have in our lives.

Let me ask you again: What is your present condition? Do you have an intimate, ongoing, and growing relationship with God? Do you depend upon the Holy Spirit to guide your path and upon God's Word to give you light? Are you ministering to others by the power of the Holy Spirit or are your activities mechanical and devoid of God's presence? Are you wise or foolish? Are you watching or sleeping?

If the midnight cry were to sound today, would you hear it? Have you truly heard the appeal to the remnant that is being presented to you through this book? Do you hear the Holy Spirit's call to be holy, turn away from the spirit of the world, and consecrate yourself to the Lord?

If Christ were to come tonight, would you be caught up with Him or left on earth in the tribulation? Christ is coming soon! If you are not sure that Christ will take you at His appearing, I invite you to pray the following prayer with me:

Heavenly Father, with all my heart, I repent for being spiritually asleep, not watching, not praying, and not having an intimate relationship with You. Please forgive me if, as You have tried to process me through the shakings we are experiencing on earth, I have given up in discouragement or despair or if I have been filled with resentment or bitterness that has pulled me away from Your presence and out of relationship with You. Today, I make a decision to forgive all past and present offenses people have committed against me. I surrender to Your processing and allow it to form me, mature me, and prepare me to be part of the bride of Christ, which is without spot or wrinkle and eagerly awaits Your coming.

Holy Spirit, fill me with Your presence and power until I am overflowing. Open my spiritual eyes and ears, purify my heart, cleanse my life of all sin, separate me from the world, and deliver me from spiritual laziness. Purify my mind from thoughts that distract me from seeking You, diminish my faith, and separate me from You. Lord Jesus Christ, give me the grace to be watchful in prayer, to seek You in spiritual intimacy, and to evangelize with a sense of urgency to prepare the way for Your appearing. I love You, and I join the cry of the Spirit that says, "Come, Lord Jesus!"

THE COMING OF THE LORD AND THE SURVIVAL OF THE CHURCH IS TIED TO THE WATCHFULNESS AND PRAYERS OF BELIEVERS.

SUMMARY

- The Old Testament uses marriage imagery to depict the relationship between God and Israel. The New Testament depicts a betrothal between Christ and the church; this marriage has not yet taken place.

- As the remnant church grows in love and faith so it can be the bride of Christ, it will also develop purer worship.

- The parable of the wise and foolish virgins reveals the state of the church today.

- In the parable, the bridegroom denotes Christ, the ten virgins represent the church, the lamps symbolize the Word of God, and the oil signifies the Holy Spirit and His power.

- Five of the virgins are characterized as foolish because they did not carry enough oil with them to replenish their lamps. When the bridegroom comes, they are not ready for his arrival. Even after they go and obtain more oil, they are refused entrance into the wedding feast. These foolish virgins represent Christians who do not have a deep relationship with God, are not continuously filled with the Holy Spirit, and will be left behind at the rapture.

- The moral to the story is the following: *"Watch therefore, for you know neither the day nor the hour in which the Son of Man is coming"* (Matthew 25:13).

- Without the Holy Spirit, the activity of the church and individual believers is mechanical and empty of God's presence. The church merely becomes a religious institution rather than the house of God.

- Much of the church today is asleep because it is exhausted from being preoccupied with the cares of life. It is spiritually lukewarm, passive, indifferent, uncommitted, insensitive, dry, blind, and even spiritually dead.

+ The bride is the portion of the church that is awake, alert, obedient, committed, holy, passionate, and strong. As it watches and prays, it is filled with the Spirit, with God's presence, and with heavenly glory and power.

+ The remnant bride prepares the way for the coming of the Bridegroom. The bride preaches the gospel with a sense of urgency and manifests God's power with miracles, signs, and wonders.

+ The "midnight cry" is the Bridegroom's call to the remnant bride. It is a call to holiness, consecration, and separation for Him. The midnight cry signifies the turning point between night and day, and therefore it represents change.

+ When the bride is removed from the earth, the Holy Spirit will also be removed as a supernatural influence and restraint against evil in the world.

+ To qualify as the remnant bride, we must allow ourselves to be processed during the shakings we are experiencing on the earth, be continuously filled with the Holy Spirit, and watch and pray until Christ comes.

SIGNS OF THE TIMES TESTIMONIES

SUPERNATURAL EVANGELISM

Albert Escoto of the United States is a dynamic, end-time evangelist whom Christ uses powerfully. Through the vision of King Jesus Ministry and the personal training of his spiritual father, Apostle Maldonado, he has been able to see the glory of God manifested in his life and in the lives of countless people he ministers to on the streets.

I believe that what God loves most are people's souls. Therefore, I have a passion to look for lost souls and bring them to Christ. When I was converted, God restored my life and gave me peace in my heart. He brought me out of alcoholism so that

I could help deliver other people who have this addiction. One day, I borrowed a car to give five people a ride to church. That day, God freed them all from alcoholism and drugs.

My wife and I frequently go out into the streets searching for those who are lost and bringing them to the light of God. We have seen cases of people who needed the Lord as much as we did. As we have ministered, the Lord has delivered thousands of people. We have witnessed all kinds of miracles and transformations in people's lives. Many people only needed a moment in God's presence to experience His touch.

Let me tell you how the Lord ministered to three particular women. One woman had been a prostitute for eight years and had been abusing alcohol and drugs for seventeen years. Another woman had participated in a gang for seven years and was a drug addict. A third woman was unable to conceive a baby. We brought them to a meeting at our House of Peace, and each one was completely set free, healed, and restored. Christ delivered them!

God's glory is being manifested over His people. We can see that He wants all those whom we meet on the streets to know Him and His kingdom. We are so thankful for what the Lord is doing through supernatural evangelism.

Nicky van der Westhuizen is a youth pastor in South Africa. His church is under the spiritual covering of King Jesus Ministry, and they are currently experiencing a radical evangelistic movement. Christ is gathering His remnant from the ends of the earth!

Essentially, ever since we connected with King Jesus Ministry, our church has been growing, especially among the youth. King Jesus's youth pastor, Pastor Joshua, has given us strategies for growth. This year, we have seen a shaking, and in just seven months, the numbers of young people in our church have doubled.

But that's not all. People don't just come into the church. They are activated to take what they've received out into the streets! This has never happened before in our ministry. And it's not as if we are seeing one or two people saved. One night, about twenty of us went out to evangelize, and in under twenty minutes, a hundred people were saved. There were also twenty-four miracles, which have been documented. In one example, a man was in a wheelchair in the middle of a shopping mall, and when some of our leaders went to pray for him, he stood up, completely healed!

One of the young people who is only twelve years old asked his teacher if she knew Jesus. She told him she was Catholic and that she was going to ask the priest. He replied, "Don't ask your priest. Ask me. Jesus is alive!" Then and there, he guided her to accept Jesus as her Lord. We have seen God move radically in every area of our ministry, but He has especially been lifting the youth of our country. We are so grateful for what He is doing and will continue to do!

CHAPTER 7

OCCUPY UNTIL HE COMES

One of the most controversial topics in the church is the role of believers in the end times. What, exactly, should we be doing while we wait for Christ's return? What does the Lord expect from the bride He comes to claim? With all the troubles in our world, should we just crawl into a cave and stay there until the end? Or should we continue to live, study, work, and develop?

This topic has given rise to several theological schools of thought. Some people believe that Jesus's return is still quite a ways off. They conclude that there is no immediate urgency and we have plenty of time to evangelize and complete God's work. Others say that because Christ is coming back soon, we do not need to progress any further in either our natural or spiritual lives; we merely need to wait for Him to return. Biblically, both of these approaches are incorrect. If, in God's purposes, Jesus does delay in coming, we should still diligently prepare for His return, just as the Lord exhorted us to do. And if Jesus *will be* returning soon, we need to prepare ourselves with an even greater sense of urgency.

The idea that we don't need to take any action because Jesus will be coming back shortly is an escapist mentality that denies the reality of the world in which we live and its need for redemption. It is not enough for *us* to be saved. God still loves those who do not yet know Him, and He longs for them to become part of His remnant bride. Such a spirit of escapism prevents believers from doing what Christ has called them to do during these last days. It keeps the church from growing and expanding. Wherever there is an escapist mindset, Christians don't live as the light of the world (see Matthew 5:14); they don't multiply in numbers of people saved, healed, and delivered; and they don't progress in their own personal lives because they think, "Why should I bother to attend school, advance in my vocation, or develop plans for evangelism if Christ is coming soon?"

DEVELOP A KINGDOM MENTALITY

Yet, in these last days, our heavenly Father wants us to develop a kingdom outlook, a "now" mentality that anticipates Jesus's return and prepares the way for His appearing. The apostles in the early church believed that Jesus was coming back in their generation. How did they respond? They preached continuously. They exhorted Christians to live holy lives and take the message of the gospel to others. However, in the first century, the end-time signs that Jesus described had yet to be fulfilled. Today's generation of believers can know with great certainty that Christ's appearance in the clouds is imminent—not just because we believe this to be the case, but because the signs are being fulfilled. Jesus is coming soon! He may even return in this very decade.

In previous chapters, we looked at end-time signs that are currently being fulfilled or will shortly be fulfilled, including signs in the physical realm like extreme weather patterns caused by climate change. I want to mention a corresponding sign: devastating, wide-ranging brush fires. During 2019–2020, unprecedented fires burned in Australia after more than two years of major drought. By the beginning of March 2020, more than 12.6 million hectares (31.1 million acres) had burned, and thirty-three people had died. It has been estimated that over a billion animals perished.[71] In New South Wales alone, at least 2,400 homes were destroyed.[72] NASA reported that "by Jan. 8, the smoke had travelled halfway around Earth, crossing South America.... The smoke is expected to make at least one full circuit around the globe, returning once again to the skies over Australia."[73] Many people in Australia prayed for rain, but when the rain did come, it caused flooding and mudslides and prompted fears of river contamination that would threaten animal species.[74]

The turmoil occurring in nature is due to the imminent return of the Lord. Creation groans to be redeemed from the curse it has suffered since the fall of mankind:

> For the earnest expectation of the creation eagerly waits for the revealing of the sons of God. For the creation was subjected to futility, not willingly, but because of Him who subjected it in hope; because the creation itself also will be delivered from the bondage of corruption into the glorious liberty of the children of God. (Romans 8:19–21)

This type of turmoil will not end anytime soon. We will repeatedly hear that another terrible situation is happening somewhere on the planet. While one country is dealing with uncontrolled wildfires, another will be dealing with floodwaters. While one nation grapples with a deadly disease, another will be engulfed in civil war. As we discussed earlier, many countries—not only developing countries but also

---

71. Joel Werner and Suzannah Lyons, "The Size of Australia's Bushfire Crisis Captured in Five Big Numbers," Australian Broadcasting Corporation (ABC), March 4, 2020, https://www.abc.net.au/news/science/2020-03-05/bushfire-crisis-five-big-numbers/12007716.

72. Bill Chappell, "Officials in Australia's New South Wales Celebrate: 'All Fires Are Now Contained,'" National Public Radio (NPR), February 13, 2020, https://www.npr.org/2020/02/13/805616731/officials-in-australias-new-south-wales-celebrate-all-fires-are-now-contained.

73. "NASA Animates World Path of Smoke and Aerosols from Australian Fires," NASA, January 9, 2020, https://www.nasa.gov/feature/goddard/2020/nasa-animates-world-path-of-smoke-and-aerosols-from-australian-fires.

74. "'Triple Whammy': Drought, Fires and Floods Push Australian Rivers into Crisis," The Guardian, February 12, 2020, https://www.theguardian.com/environment/2020/feb/12/triple-whammy-hits-push-australian-rivers-crisis.

developed ones—are going through serious economic crises. Stock markets are collapsing, and governments are struggling to stabilize financial conditions. Such end-time events have the ability to incapacitate entire cities and nations. In just a short period, a nation that has been a world power might become like a third-world country, and no one will be able to stop it. We cannot sit around waiting during these end times! We must do what the Lord has called us to do before He comes!

Some people think their salvation is purely an individual matter between them and God, with no thought as to the spiritual condition of others. However, from God's perspective, if a believer attends church yet does nothing to spread the gospel and expand the kingdom of God on earth, they are sinning. As we will explore more fully in the next section, Jesus calls us to *"do business"* (Luke 19:13), or *"occupy"* (KJV), until He comes. We know that in Matthew 24, Jesus made prophetic declarations about the signs of the end times. In chapter 25, He began speaking in parables because He wanted His disciples to respond to the messages He had just given them. We cannot merely hear Jesus's warnings and admonitions; we must act on them. (See James 1:22–24.)

In chapter 6 of this book, we explored one of the two parables Jesus gave in Matthew 25, that of the wise and foolish virgins. This parable depicts the end-time church and the remnant bride, demonstrating the importance of vigil and prayer. (See Matthew 25:1–13.) The other symbolic story, which we will review in this chapter, is the parable of the talents, which addresses the need for stewardship and productivity on the part of believers. (See verses 14–30.)

What these parables have in common is that, although the people in the stories don't know *when* the bridegroom or the lord will come back, they know that he *will* return. In the first parable, the virgins have to keep watch for the bridegroom's appearance. In the second, the servants have to work to multiply their lord's goods so they can give an account of their stewardship when he returns.

We are in a similar position today. We do not know the day or hour *when* Jesus will return, but we do know for certain that He *is* coming.

We don't have all the time in the world to prepare for that day! We don't know if we have one, two, five, ten, twenty, or a hundred years—much less a day or two—before He appears. We only know that He is coming soon. Since His return is imminent, we do not want to run the risk of being left behind, either for lack of "oil" (the presence and power of the Holy Spirit in our lives) or for neglecting our spiritual responsibilities.

> **TO HAVE A KINGDOM MENTALITY IS TO LIVE AS IF CHRIST WILL RETURN TOMORROW AND TO PLAN AS IF HE WILL RETURN A HUNDRED YEARS FROM NOW. IN EITHER CASE, WE MUST PREPARE NOW!**

THE PARABLE OF THE TALENTS

To understand the parable of the talents, we need to read the whole passage and then discuss various aspects of the story.

For the kingdom of heaven is like a man traveling to a far country, who called his own servants and delivered his goods to them. And to one he gave five talents, to another two, and to another one, to each according to his own ability; and immediately he went on a journey. Then he who had received the five talents went and traded with them, and made another five talents. And likewise he who had received two gained two more also. But he who had received one went and dug in the ground, and hid his lord's money. After a long time the lord of those servants came and settled accounts with them. So he who had received five talents came and brought five other talents, saying, "Lord, you delivered to me five talents; look, I have gained five more talents besides them." His lord said to him, "Well done, good and faithful servant; you were faithful over a few things,

I will make you ruler over many things. Enter into the joy of your lord." He also who had received two talents came and said, "Lord, you delivered to me two talents; look, I have gained two more talents besides them." His lord said to him, "Well done, good and faithful servant; you have been faithful over a few things, I will make you ruler over many things. Enter into the joy of your lord." Then he who had received the one talent came and said, "Lord, I knew you to be a hard man, reaping where you have not sown, and gathering where you have not scattered seed. And I was afraid, and went and hid your talent in the ground. Look, there you have what is yours." But his lord answered and said to him, "You wicked and lazy servant, you knew that I reap where I have not sown, and gather where I have not scattered seed. So you ought to have deposited my money with the bankers, and at my coming I would have received back my own with interest. So take the talent from him, and give it to him who has ten talents. For to everyone who has, more will be given, and he will have abundance; but from him who does not have, even what he has will be taken away. And cast the unprofitable servant into the outer darkness. There will be weeping and gnashing of teeth."

(Matthew 25:14–30)

GOD'S STEWARDS

The parable of the talents is based on the "law of increase," which is a kingdom principle. In the parable, a man appoints three of his servants as stewards. A steward is someone who oversees the money, goods, or household of another. When the Lord Jesus ascended to heaven, He entrusted the administration of His kingdom on earth—His ministry, message, church, gifts, and power—to His disciples. Believers in the twenty-first century are entrusted with the same stewardship.

"After a long time the lord of those servants came and settled accounts with them" (Matthew 25:19). When Jesus returns, He will ask us to account for what we have done with the resources He has given us, just as the master in the parable asks his servants to account for the goods

over which he gave them stewardship. We will have to give an account of our life, family, ministry, occupation, spiritual gifts, resources, money, time, faith, and so on. From this parable, we learn that we do not own anything for ourselves. Everything we have belongs to Jesus, who is the Lord of all. He is the Owner, and we are His servants who are called to administer His goods.

We must truly understand that we will have to explain to Jesus what we have done with everything He has given us during our lifetime. No one wants to be held accountable for what they have done; it is not something that comes naturally to us. For this reason, we need to learn to walk in the fear of God. *"And if you call on the Father, who without partiality judges according to each one's work, conduct yourselves throughout the time of your stay here in fear"* (1 Peter 1:17).

Many believers want Christ to come back, but they don't think about the fact that, when He returns to earth, there will be a day of reckoning. At the judgment, the Lord will confront each of us, asking, "What have you done with My goods? Have you been faithful with what I gave you? Have you produced anything with it? Have you multiplied it? Where is the fruit?" The Lord will ask us question after question.

We will be held accountable by God for the way we have lived our lives because the kingdom is not a game, nor is it for people who want to act independently, who won't submit to proper authority. In the parable of the talents, the servant who was cowardly, unproductive, and irresponsible was rejected and cast into *"outer darkness."* (See Matthew 25:30.) Again, we must develop a healthy fear of God and recognize that He may reject us if we disregard the essence of His kingdom message and what He has called us to do.

DO GOD'S BUSINESS

In the parable of the minas, which is a variation of the parable of the talents, the master's command is a little more explicit: *"So he called ten of his servants, delivered to them ten minas, and said to them, 'Do business till I come'"* (Luke 19:13). In this narrative, as in the parable of the talents, when the lord entrusted his wealth to his servants, his intention was that they would work with it and multiply it—that is, "*do business*" with it.

In both of these parables, Jesus was speaking symbolically about what Christians should be doing before He returns. It is interesting that He used the phrase "*do business*," which refers to making transactions to earn a profit. The owner of the minas expected his servants to actively multiply his wealth while he was away. Jesus was telling His disciples that they should engage in His enterprises and multiply them by investing in them and working toward their growth. In Matthew 25:16–17, we see that the faithful servants made a profit with the talents they had received: "*Then he who had received the five talents went and traded with them, and made another five talents. And likewise he who had received two gained two more also.*"

Let us remember that when Jesus was on earth, He was focused on doing His Father's business. "*And He said to them, "Why did you seek Me? Did you not know that I must be about My Father's business?*" (Luke 2:49). What is the Father's business? It is to proclaim God's Word; pray; fast; multiply and expand His kingdom on earth; bring salvations, healings, and miracles; cast out demons, restore families; and be productive and fruitful in the church and in the marketplace, just as Jesus, His disciples, and the early church did.

A PERSON WHO IS STAGNANT, NOT PRODUCING OR MULTIPLYING WHAT THE LORD HAS GIVEN THEM, IS SINNING BEFORE GOD.

These are times when we must be busy doing what the Lord has commanded us to do—and with a sense of urgency. (See Philippians

2:12–13.) While we should never be casual, cowardly, or negligent about our stewardship of God's resources, this is especially true in the end times. In the business world, most employees won't retain their positions or advance in their careers if they are unproductive in their jobs because they are not doing what they were hired for. Our Lord expects us to be productive by engaging in the Father's business and bearing fruit for His kingdom.

"BE FRUITFUL AND MULTIPLY"

The parable of the talents does not present a new or unusual concept when it speaks of "doing business" for the Lord. Rather, this has been God's plan from the beginning. *"Be fruitful and multiply"* was the Creator's original mandate for human beings: *"Then God blessed them, and God said to them, 'Be fruitful and multiply; fill the earth and subdue it; have dominion over the fish of the sea, over the birds of the air, and over every living thing that moves on the earth'"* (Genesis 1:28).

No one has an excuse before God to remain inactive or unfruitful. The Lord has given each believer one or more "talents," or gifts, and expects us to use them. A talent can be a spiritual endowment or a natural ability. It can be money, resources, possessions, objects, places, wealth, faith, anointing, blessings, or people. No matter what type of talents we have, or how many, Christ has entrusted them to us to be developed and multiplied so we can present the results to Him when He returns. God has given us so many good things. What are you doing with what He has given you?

EVEN IF YOU DECIDE YOU WANT TO BE THE OWNER RATHER THAN THE STEWARD OF WHAT GOD HAS GIVEN YOU, YOU ARE NEVERTHELESS RESPONSIBLE TO HIM AND WILL STILL HAVE TO GIVE AN ACCOUNT FOR THE WAY YOU HAVE LIVED YOUR LIFE.

OCCUPY

"So he called ten of his servants, delivered to them ten minas, and said to them, 'Do business till I come'" (Luke 19:13). The King James Version uses the word *"occupy"* instead of *"do business."* The Greek word means "to busy oneself with," "to trade," or "to occupy." The English term *occupy* comes from the Middle English *occupien,* meaning "to take possession of, hold, inhabit, take up space in, fill, keep busy." This word can have a military connotation, referring to an army taking charge of a conquered territory. As we await Christ's return, we must enter and occupy the territories God has given us to administer on behalf of His kingdom.

Most preachers who talk about the coming of the Lord don't mention our responsibility to be at our Father's business by occupying the territories He has given us. Again, the reason many Christians are not acting on this responsibility is that they have an end-time mentality of escapism instead of a mindset of ongoing service to God.

As we "do business," or "occupy," in anticipation of the Lord's return, we must not lose sight of the fact that we are engaged in a spiritual war. When we forget this, two things occur: we do not produce fruit, and we give up. When an army is at war, no soldier can be lazy or unproductive. War keeps us on our toes because people's lives are at stake.

The fact is, when a believer commits to being productive, expanding, and multiplying for God's kingdom, Satan will immediately intensify his warfare against them. He will seek to incapacitate that person or even take their life. *"For we do not wrestle against flesh and blood, but against principalities, against powers, against the rulers of the darkness of this age, against spiritual hosts of wickedness in the heavenly places"* (Ephesians 6:12). The good news is that Christ has already defeated Satan, and He fights for us. Jesus paid the price for our spiritual freedom and empowerment when He came to earth, died on the cross, and rose again. (See Romans 8:31–37.) Heaven has given us the resources we need to fight spiritual battles against the enemy, starting with the indwelling presence of the Holy Spirit. We have the Spirit's power, the Word of God, the name of Jesus, and the blood of the Lamb to execute the victory Christ won.

As the time for the Lord's coming draws near, let us take more territory, win more souls, and make more disciples. Let us expand and be productive for the kingdom. When Jesus returns, He must find us watching, praying, and actively doing the Father's business.

THE PURPOSE OF ANY WAR IS VICTORY, THEN OCCUPATION, AND FINALLY EXPANSION.

DON'T BE A SPIRITUAL THIEF!

One of the biggest problems in the church today is that we tolerate unproductiveness, as if the principles of the kingdom have changed. However, as Jesus told us, whatever does not produce fruit is cut off. *"Every branch in Me that does not bear fruit [God] takes away; and every branch that bears fruit He prunes, that it may bear more fruit"* (John 15:2).

In the parable of the talents, the master dealt very harshly with the servant who had produced nothing with what he had been given:

Then he who had received the one talent came and said, "Lord, I knew you to be a hard man, reaping where you have not sown, and gathering where you have not scattered seed. And I was afraid, and went and hid your talent in the ground. Look, there you have what is yours." But his lord answered and said to him, "You wicked and lazy servant, you knew that I reap where I have not sown, and gather where I have not scattered seed. So you ought to have deposited my money with the bankers, and at my coming I would have received back my own with interest. So take the talent from him, and give it to him who has ten talents. For to everyone who has, more will be given, and he will have abundance; but from him who does not have, even what he has will be taken away. (Matthew 25:24–29)

The lord calls the third servant *"wicked and lazy."* The Greek word translated *"lazy"* can also be rendered as "tardy," "indolent," or "irksome." We must be careful not to develop the same characteristics by neglecting to faithfully serve God and His kingdom. Someone who is unproductive for the kingdom could be considered a "spiritual thief."

The servant in the parable was unfruitful. In his defense, he says that his lack of action was due to his fear, but the lord calls him *"unprofitable"*: *"And cast the unprofitable servant into the outer darkness. There will be weeping and gnashing of teeth"* (Matthew 25:30). The servant may have been paralyzed by fear, but this was still not a valid excuse for him to do nothing with his talent. The Scriptures tell us that neither thieves nor cowards will enter the kingdom of God. (See 1 Corinthians 6:9–10; Revelation 21:8.) Whenever we are afraid to do something that God has called us to do, we must remind ourselves of these Scriptures and trust the Holy Spirit to work through us:

These things I have spoken to you, that in Me you may have peace. In the world you will have tribulation; but be of good cheer, I have overcome the world. (John 16:33)

For it is God who works in you both to will and to do for His good pleasure. (Philippians 2:13)

For God has not given us a spirit of fear, but of power and of love and of a sound mind. (2 Timothy 1:7)

We need to produce right where we are now, whether it is at home, at work, at church, at our ministry, or anywhere else. We must walk in the fear of God, recognizing that one day we will be judged and will have to give an account of what we have done with the gifts we have received from the Lord.

Allow me to conclude this section by telling you something that is not preached about in most churches: unproductiveness leads to debt!

The more you refrain from giving of your talents and resources to serve God, the more debt you will have. This debt may take the form of vocational, financial, material, emotional, or spiritual lack. In contrast, being faithful in giving is the key to being productive in the kingdom because to give is to sow, and what you sow will always bear corresponding fruit. (See Galatians 6:7–8.)

> **UNPRODUCTIVENESS AND LAZINESS ARE BAD STEWARDSHIP. BOTH WILL COST YOU YOUR PLACE IN THE KINGDOM, LEAD YOU INTO DEBT, AND KEEP YOU ON EARTH AT THE RAPTURE.**

STEPS TO BECOMING A PROFITABLE SERVANT

So, how can we become profitable servants of God? Let's look at several practical ways we can be productive in the kingdom as we wait for the coming of the Lord Jesus.

BE IN YOUR ASSIGNED PLACE

You did not choose Me, but I chose you and appointed you that you should go and bear fruit, and that your fruit should remain, that whatever you ask the Father in My name He may give you.

(John 15:16)

The place to which the Lord has assigned us is the only place where we will be fruitful. It is where we will be able to progress in fulfilling our purpose and secure the resources we need to complete it. No soldier fighting a battle chooses their own assignment. Rather, they receive their assignment and position from those who are in command. God is our Commander-in-Chief, and He has assigned us to a particular time, place, ethnicity, people, and culture. He does so with the expectation that we will "do business" there and occupy the territory in order to expand His kingdom. Again, only in this territory, and no other, will we be able to flourish.

There is a place in business, the arts, music, sports, science, banking, the family, or another area waiting for each of us. We have a post that we are responsible for until Christ returns. We must be vigilant there, not elsewhere. Note that God may lead us in various directions during our lifetimes, so we always need to follow the Spirit's leading regarding where He is positioning us. Wherever that is, we will fulfill the overall calling He has given us, and we must be faithful there. In ancient times, if a Roman soldier left his post, it cost him his life. In the spiritual world, neglecting our assignment could result in our being left behind when Jesus appears.

As an apostle of God, my job is to keep watch in the post God has given me and to help other people understand their assignments, even directing them to their particular posts. If you are a doctor, accountant, lawyer, businessperson, apostle, pastor, or evangelist, that is your post, and you must fulfill your kingdom assignment. Remember that you cannot be in the kingdom and fail to produce fruit, so ask the Holy Spirit to reveal your assignment and then begin to watch, pray, and produce from there.

ANY TERRITORY YOU ARE ASSIGNED TO RELATES TO YOUR PURPOSE.

KNOW AND FULFILL YOUR PURPOSE

When we find our purpose, we also find our prosperity because God provides for the fulfillment of any purpose that He Himself has designed. Many people are unable to prosper and, therefore, live in poverty because they are striving to fulfill a purpose for which they were not created. People won't find their prosperity if they are engaged in something that is not connected to the reason for which God made them. To understand our purpose, we need to know our heavenly Father intimately through prayer, where He reveals our identity and, with it, the idea He had in mind when He gave us life. If we know God's plan for us and follow it, we will not remain sterile or fruitless. Instead, we will multiply the gifts we have received so that we can present our fruit to the Lord upon His return.

INVEST IN WHAT IS ETERNAL

Anything that is eternal will increase and impact generations. We must realize that not everything we sow has eternal impact. We need God's wisdom to invest in what will last. Without this wisdom, we may think we're engaged in the right pursuits but, in reality, we may be sowing into what is merely temporary and will pass away. To invest in what is eternal, we have to sow something that has the power to multiply and to positively affect the destiny of people and places. For example, we can invest in the gospel, people's salvation, the nation of Israel, the manifestation of the Holy Spirit's power, and so forth—always through the guidance and wisdom of God's Spirit.

We must keep in mind that the condition for experiencing increase from God in any area of our life is to use what He has given us. Everything the Lord imparts to us is for kingdom purposes. Again, our stewardship is measured by what we do with our gifts while we are on earth as we anticipate Jesus's return. God promises crowns to those who have invested their lives in what is eternal. (See 2 Timothy 4:8; James 1:12; Revelation 2:10.)

EVERY INCREASE SHOULD BE FOR THE SAKE OF THE KINGDOM.

BE SENT OUT

As I mentioned previously, it is vital for us to know the particular territory to which God has assigned us because it is connected with our purpose and calling. Moreover, we need to recognize that authority rests upon the person who is appointed to a territory. Thus, we have to be properly sent out to our place of assignment in order to exercise authority in it. This is why, even if we understand our purpose, assignment, and territory, we still need someone in spiritual authority over us to endorse us and send us out.

After these things **the Lord appointed seventy others also, and sent them** *two by two before His face into every city and place where He Himself was about to go.* (Luke 10:1)

As they ministered to the Lord and fasted, the Holy Spirit said, "Now separate to Me Barnabas and Saul for the work to which I have called them." Then, having fasted and prayed, and laid hands on them, they sent them away. (Acts 13:2–3)

Everyone who is sent by God is empowered by Him. Believers who are commissioned by Jesus have the highest level of spiritual authority in their sphere of influence. The angels of the Lord walk with them and guard them. By contrast, those who have not been sent lack authority and cannot command evil spiritual principalities and powers. These principalities and powers recognize the difference between someone whom God has sent and someone who has merely arrived on their own and is working according to their own power. (See Acts 19:11–17.)

Today, we see many casualties of spiritual warfare involving people who either were not sent or are trying to work in an area to which they have not been called. These are also the reasons why many Christians, churches, and ministries fail to grow. It is not that they aren't anointed but rather that their authority is not recognized in the spiritual realm. You can pray and fast but still not accomplish what you set out to if you are not sent. However, when you are sent out by God and the spiritual leaders in your life, even the principalities and powers will recognize your authority and obey your commands.

When I send people into ministry, I recognize them in front of the congregation because in addition to knowing that this will empower them in the presence of God and in the spiritual realm, I also understand that the church must witness their calling and commission. Furthermore, anyone who is given a commission has already been processed by God. This means they have matured in their character so they can handle the anointing, the gifts, the power, and the grace that God has entrusted to them to multiply in their territory. Remember that maturity is one of the requirements for being part of the remnant bride that prepares the way for the coming of Christ and stands ready to go with Him in the rapture. Therefore, in order to pursue our God-given purpose and occupy a territory for the kingdom, we must be willing to submit to a process of character development that will lead us to become commissioned.

> **WHEREVER GOD SENDS US, HE GIVES US A TERRITORY AND THE AUTHORITY TO OPERATE IN IT. ONLY UNDER THESE CONDITIONS CAN WE BE FRUITFUL.**

BUSY WITH OUR FATHER'S BUSINESS

In this chapter, we have examined a crucial truth relating to Christian discipleship: before Jesus ascended to heaven, He left instructions that every believer should make good use of the gifts and abilities God has given them. He expects each of us to be productive until He returns. We must be busy with our Father's business, just as Jesus was always engaged in the Father's business while He was on earth. Jesus wants to see fruit in the form of kingdom expansion, souls won, healings manifested, and so on.

Are you prepared to give Jesus an account of your life? Do you know that you are in your place of assignment? If so, are you keeping busy there? Are you doing the Father's business? Are you being a good steward of His goods? Have you multiplied your gifts? Have you expanded the kingdom? In these last days, we cannot crawl into a cave and do nothing, giving the excuse that "Jesus is coming tomorrow." The Lord was clear about His intentions when He spoke to His disciples, and His words are just as clear for us, too: "I want you to do business with your talents. Be productive until I return." If you feel that this challenge is for you, please pray the following prayer with me:

Lord Jesus, I ask You to reveal my purpose and place of assignment so that I may be a good soldier and occupy the territory You have put in my charge. Empower me to fulfill this purpose. I recognize that You have given me gifts and talents to use on this earth until You come back for Your remnant bride. I do not want to be found negligent, evil, or lazy when You return and ask me to give an account of what I have done with all that You have bestowed upon me. Today, I ask You for the grace, strength, and wisdom to produce and multiply the gifts and abilities You have placed in my care. I commit to work on Your behalf and to bear much fruit for Your kingdom. Put the fear of God in me so that I will act responsibly with what You have entrusted to me. Give me a sense of end-time urgency so that I will always be on the alert, spreading the gospel wherever I go.

Lord Jesus, at Your return, may You find me watching, praying, working, and producing. May You be able to say to me, *"Well done, good and faithful servant…. Enter into the joy of your lord."* Come quickly, Lord Jesus!

SUMMARY

- One of the most controversial topics in the church is the role of believers in the end times, including what, specifically, we should be doing as we wait for Christ's return.

- This topic has given rise to various theological schools of thought, including the following: (1) Jesus's return is still quite a ways off, so there is plenty of time to preach the gospel and complete God's work with no immediate sense of urgency. (2) Jesus will return tomorrow, so we don't need to progress any further in our natural or spiritual lives (escapism theology).

- In the parable of the talents, the lord commissions three of his servants as stewards, giving them various amounts of his wealth to take charge of while he is away on a trip. Upon his return, he calls each of them to give an account of their stewardship.

- In the similar parable of the minas, to "*do business*" (Luke 19:13) refers to making transactions to earn a profit.

- The servants who received multiple talents doubled what the lord had given them. Upon his return, the master commended and rewarded them.

- The servant who received the single talent was afraid of his master. He buried his talent in the ground so that, when he was called to account for his stewardship, he merely gave the original money back to his lord without having produced any profit with it. The master treated this servant as useless, evil, and negligent. He took the one talent away from him and sent him into "*outer darkness*" (Matthew 25:30).

- Since the beginning of creation, one of God's primary commands to human beings has been, "*Be fruitful and multiply*" (Genesis 1:28).

- One of the greatest problems in the church today is that we tolerate unproductiveness.

- Unproductiveness leads to debt. This debt may take the form of vocational, financial, material, emotional, or spiritual lack.

- Some practical ways to be productive in the kingdom while awaiting Jesus's return are the following: be in your assigned place, know and fulfill your purpose, invest in what is eternal, and be sent out.

- To have a kingdom mentality means to always be producing fruit and to always be ready for Christ's arrival—whether He ultimately returns tomorrow or a hundred years from now.

SIGNS OF THE TIMES TESTIMONIES

END-TIME KINGDOM EXPANSION

Pastor Paulo Tércio Silva, from São Paulo, Brazil, has a sense of urgency to preach the gospel of the kingdom in his city, his country, and the rest of the world. He is busy implementing various evangelistic strategies, multiplying what the Father has given him and fulfilling his purpose in the territory God has assigned to him.

In our ministry, we have three main strategies for evangelism. First, on Saturdays, we go out to the train stations in São Paulo and preach the gospel to people who are traveling. We also pray for their needs. On one occasion, we met a deaf man and asked if we could pray for him. The Lord completely healed him on the spot! Another time, we saw a woman buying alcohol. When we spoke with her, she told us that she wanted to get drunk because she had fought with her husband and had decided to leave him. She also said that she had been a pastor. We preached to her and prayed for her, and she was filled with the Holy Spirit right there. Today, her marriage is restored, and she is leading her church again! In another divine appointment, we talked to a boy who was traveling on a bus, explaining to him about God's love. He told us he had never felt this love that we were talking about, so we prayed for him, and he was baptized in the Holy Spirit.

Our second strategy is to choose a street near our church and devote a month to going house by house preaching the gospel; giving words of prophecy, knowledge, and wisdom; and praying for healings. After four weeks, we ask the people who have responded to the gospel if they would like to open their home as a House of Peace, and we establish a fellowship group in one of these neighborhood homes. On one of the streets where we evangelized, we met a woman who was suffering from depression and was very sick with cancer. We started a House of Peace in her home, and she brought all her neighbors to the meeting. Today, she is free from depression, and we are believing that she will be free from cancer too.

Our third strategy is to go to a nearby shopping center every week to talk to people about Christ, pray for healings, and even cast out demons. Then, we invite those whom we meet to come to our church services. When we prayed for one woman and gave her a prophetic word concerning her wounded foot, she was healed and received Jesus into her heart. We met another woman who was blind in one eye and was scheduled for surgery. When we prayed for her, she was immediately healed also. We have shared the gospel with about fifty-five hundred people, and more than a thousand have confessed Jesus as their Lord and Savior. The most difficult obstacles to the gospel that we encounter are people's religiosity and idolatry. Some churches that operate according to these mindsets persecute other churches who are moving in the Holy Spirit. The spirit of this age is trying to confuse and separate people.

I have a burning passion in my heart to take the gospel and miracles to churches, to our city, and to all manner of people: atheists, Hindus, drug dealers, politicians, the rich, the poor, the sick. I want to reach people through art, culture, music, literature, business, and more. Kingdom expansion is urgent because there is no time to lose! Furthermore, I feel the need for holiness in the church. Unfortunately, false prophets are spreading seductive messages against the fear of God, humility, and the family. Pride will precede the fall of any church that thinks commitment to God and kingdom expansion are not crucial in these end times. Everything we need to accomplish God's purposes is available to us in the spiritual realm, but we must do His will, filled with the Holy Spirit! We have seen the Lord move in our congregation, especially in evangelism. We are waiting for Jesus's return, but we are being diligent as we wait.

Pastors Genemar and Abigaile Corpuz from Hawaii were activated by the Holy Spirit when they listened to Apostle Maldonado preach about the supernatural power of God on YouTube. Today, they are part of the remnant that prepares the way for Jesus, busily multiplying what God has given them as they await Christ's return. Pastor Abigaile testifies:

Before we connected with King Jesus Ministry, our church was stagnant and our membership fluctuated. I asked the Lord how I could experience more of His power and presence, and I told Him that I wanted more from Him. I had my computer nearby, and while I was browsing the Internet, I inadvertently came across a video of Apostle Maldonado on YouTube. He was preaching about how to be transformed by God's presence. At that moment, my prayer was answered. The Holy Spirit filled me with His presence, and I was able to experience His power.

Pastor Genemar continues:

The apostle's teachings were so different from any that I'd ever heard before that they impacted my heart. Since then, my hunger and thirst for God have increased. I asked my wife to buy Apostle Maldonado's books and told her that it was time for us to be activated in the power of the Lord. Those books led us to be transformed by the presence of God—so much so that miracles began to happen in our church. A woman had stage 4 lung cancer, but she was healed by God's power. A man was scheduled for surgery because he was suffering from diabetes and cataracts and was blind in his right eye. This man asked us to pray that the operation would be successful, but I told him I would pray for his healing. He began to cry and believe it was possible. That week, when I called him to ask about the operation, he started crying over the phone. He said that he had checked his right eye three times before the operation and was amazed to find that he could read both the large and small letters on the eye chart. The doctor could not believe the change. She asked him what he had done for his eye, and he replied that his pastor had prayed for him. The operation was canceled because he no longer needed it!

God has opened many means of communication for us to spread the message of His supernatural power. We have a radio program, and we receive calls and messages from people in various nations who have heard our broadcasts. We also broadcast our church service on the Internet. There was a woman in a hospital who had been in a coma for eight days. With the family's permission, this woman's doctors had already set a date and time to disconnect all her life-support machines because she was in a vegetative state and there wasn't any hope of recovery. However, a friend of the comatose woman was watching our service over the Internet as she sat with her in the hospital. After seeing the broadcast of our service, this friend called us and asked for prayer. The woman revived! Glory to the living God! She was resurrected by the power of the Holy Spirit!

During a missions trip, we ministered to a man in a wheelchair who could not see out of his right eye or hear out of his right ear, and he was immediately healed. Right there, we saw him walk again, and his senses began to return to normal. We also activated many believers to do miracles. In addition, our fourteen-year-old daughter has been activated and is leading the young people in our church, ministering deliverance and healing to them. We thank God for raising up this generation with a supernatural culture that gives Him glory.

CHAPTER 8

PREPARING FOR JESUS'S RETURN

The remnant bride must be ready for the coming of her Bridegroom! The Holy Spirit has revealed, and continues to reveal, how we should prepare for this climactic event. In this final chapter, I want to review several indispensable scriptural keys for our preparation that the Spirit of God has emphasized to me.

ALLOW JESUS TO PURIFY AND CONSECRATE YOU

It is Christ who prepares His bride. Jesus made complete provision for us—spiritually, emotionally, and physically—when He gave His life on our behalf. He paid the price to ransom us from sin, fully redeeming us. Now, He refines us so that He can present us to Himself as a pure bride. This is why our first step must be to respond to Jesus's process of purifying our lives. We have to do our part so that God can do His. Remember this vital revelation regarding the type of bride for whom Christ will return:

Husbands, love your wives, just as Christ also loved the church and gave Himself for her, that He might sanctify and cleanse her with the washing of water by the word, that He might present her to Himself a glorious church, not having spot or wrinkle or any such thing, but that she should be holy and without blemish. (Ephesians 5:25–27)

It is essential to understand that Christ desires a glorious, holy, and pure bride not for some arbitrary reason but because these qualities are foundational to His own nature. *"As He who called you is holy, you also be holy in all your conduct, because it is written, 'Be holy, for I am holy'"* (1 Peter 1:15–16). The Father, Son, and Spirit are glorious, holy, and pure in their essence. Christ must cleanse us of all impurities, defilements, and filth so that we may become a glorious church, suitable to be His bride. God's remnant will be innocent, unspotted, unwrinkled, and unblemished. The character of the bride will be formed according to the character of the Bridegroom. *"Till we all come to the unity of the faith and of the knowledge of the Son of God, to a perfect man, to the measure of the stature of the fullness of Christ"* (Ephesians 4:13).

> **BEING HOLY BEFORE GOD IS NOT AN OPTION BUT RATHER A COMMAND. HOLINESS PURIFIES OUR CHARACTER AND MAKES US FULLY LOYAL TO CHRIST.**

A purified church will not love sin, will not practice the works of the flesh, and will have died to sinful desires. If any member of the remnant does sin, they will be so sensitive to the Holy Spirit's gentle but firm correction that they will repent immediately and be restored. *"Pursue peace with all people, and holiness, without which no one will see the Lord"* (Hebrews 12:14).

Another aspect of the sanctified church is that it is exclusively set apart to be Christ's bride. The true remnant follows Jesus alone. It doesn't have a mixture of loyalties—a little bit of devotion to Christ, a little bit of adherence to the world, and a little bit of obedience to the devil. No, it is fully devoted to Christ!

The bride is consecrated to God and has sanctified herself to hear His voice, obey Him, and serve Him. She does not rely on human strength or man-made religious doctrines. Instead, she walks according to the Spirit's counsel and advances with His power to spread the kingdom of God. The bride is a bringer of God's glory to the earth!

Holiness, then, is the foremost mark of the remnant. Those who are members of Christ's bride are not like everyone else in the world. They are distinguished by their consecration to the Lord, which leads them to live their lives separated from sin and worldliness as they dedicate themselves to God's service. However, this does not mean that they shun going into the world. No, they live, work, and witness in the world. However, as they do, they shine the light of Jesus amid the darkness. They fight for justice, defend the innocent, heal the sick, liberate the oppressed, and preach the message of the kingdom that Jesus has entrusted to them. The Holy Spirit is calling all members of the remnant bride to fully dedicate themselves to Christ so they may prepare the way for His coming.

> **GOD'S FIRST CALL TO HIS PEOPLE IS TO BE HOLY AND SEPARATED FOR HIM. THEREFORE, THE FOREMOST MARK OF THE REMNANT BRIDE IS HOLINESS.**

The members of the end-time remnant are also filled with faith, taking God at His Word, believing everything He has declared and

202 JESUS IS COMING SOON

promised. It should not be difficult to recognize or identify the holy remnant that arises as a glorious bride—always alive, active, growing, manifesting the Father, driving the enemy out of the territory he has usurped, and extending God's kingdom wherever she goes.

KEEP VIGILANT

As has been noted throughout this book, the true bride vigilantly watches and prays. Shakings and other end-time signs are evident in the world around us, and it would be precarious for us to overlook or ignore them. We cannot allow ourselves to become spiritually indifferent, distracted, or drowsy. Again, we need to be focused on our purpose, always serving God, attentive to the signs, and living in expectation of the Lord's coming.

"Watch therefore, and pray always that you may be counted worthy to escape all these things that will come to pass, and to stand before the Son of Man" (Luke 21:36). If we want to be raptured with the remnant bride, we must keep alert. If we do not watch, we may fall into temptation and miss Jesus's coming. We can remain watchful through continual prayer, which will also produce spiritual breakthroughs in our lives. As I wrote in my book *Breakthrough Prayer,*

In the natural world, momentum is the force, power, or propulsion that an object gains while it is in motion. During momentum, there is a point at which an object reaches its maximum impulse. When a long jump athlete reaches his full momentum, he gives his best jump. Similarly, in the spiritual realm, when we continue to pray, we reach the precise measure of accumulated prayers that brings the spiritual atmosphere into its fullness, producing a supernatural impulse that brings the breakthrough.[75]

Let us maintain our momentum in prayer until Jesus returns. Let us make sure that a supernatural impulse, generated by continual

---

75. Guillermo Maldonado, *Breakthrough Prayer* (New Kensington, PA: Whitaker House, 2018), 167–68.

intercession, is working within us at His appearing. This cannot occur if we are spiritually asleep or lack the oil of the Spirit!

MAINTAIN A SENSE OF URGENCY

"But know this, that in the last days perilous times will come" (2 Timothy 3:1). We have to wake up and pay attention to what is happening in the world! We must see the signs that point to the reality that Jesus is coming back. We need an awareness of God's "now," an understanding of how the Lord is working, what end-time events are occurring, and why. This will lead us to conduct ourselves with a sense of urgency in everything we do.

Much of the church today lacks a sense of urgency regarding Jesus's return. If we are awake, watching, and praying, if we are fully aware that the time of Christ's coming is near, then people will perceive the sense of urgency in our voices and our actions as we preach, teach, minister, serve, and work. Remember, we do not have all the time in the world to do God's will on earth. Time is short!

CULTIVATE AN INTIMATE RELATIONSHIP WITH GOD

Another essential mark of the remnant bride is that she has a progressive, continuous, and intimate relationship with God. This is a key point of preparation for Christ's return. Keep in mind that in Jesus's parable of the ten virgins, the five foolish virgins' major deficiency was their shortage of oil, representing a lack of intimacy with God, ability to hear His voice, anointing, and power. As a result, the foolish virgins missed the bridegroom's arrival and were excluded from the wedding. When they later sought entrance, the bridegroom replied with these devastating words: *"Assuredly, I say to you, I do not know you"* (Matthew 25:12).

There are Christians who have never been intimate with the Lord, even though they have healed the sick, cast out demons, prophesied, and much more. Let me repeat Jesus's warning to those who think they can enter the kingdom without having a close relationship with God:

Not everyone who says to Me, "Lord, Lord," shall enter the kingdom of heaven, but he who does the will of My Father in heaven. Many will say to Me in that day, "Lord, Lord, have we not prophesied in Your name, cast out demons in Your name, and done many wonders in Your name?" And then I will declare to them, "I never knew you; depart from Me, you who practice lawlessness!"

(Matthew 7:21–23)

▌ TO HAVE A CLOSE RELATIONSHIP WITH GOD, WE MUST INVEST QUALITY TIME WITH HIM.

How can we come to know the Father intimately? Through earnest prayer and a heart that is open and ready to listen. Prayer is the place where God reveals Himself and entrusts His secrets to us. In prayer, we learn what God is doing and what He is about to do. *"Surely the Lord GOD does nothing, unless He reveals His secret to His servants the prophets"* (Amos 3:7).

In essence, when people don't want to pray, they show they are not interested in a relationship with God. They have not received the revelation of what will happen when they relate to the Father in an intimate way. Jesus spent hours in His heavenly Father's presence because that was where He connected with the Father and received His identity, power, grace, and wisdom. Through prayer, Jesus received revelation about future events in His life, such as His death and resurrection and what would come about as a result of them. From His relationship with the Father, Jesus drew the strength and conviction He needed to endure the agony of crucifixion and to emerge victorious over sin, Satan, and death.

Unless we pray, we cannot have such an intimate relationship with God or receive revelation from Him. If we are not praying, we will certainly miss Jesus's appearing because we will be asleep, unable to hear or see in the spiritual realm. Communication is the life of any relationship; when communication stops, the relationship ceases. This truth applies not only to our relationships with other people, but also to our relationship with God. If we stop praying, we will cease to know the Lord, and this will lead to dire consequences:

> *If anyone does not abide in Me, he is cast out as a branch and is withered; and they gather them and throw them into the fire, and they are burned. If you abide in Me, and My words abide in you, you will ask what you desire, and it shall be done for you.*
>
> (John 15:6–7)

When we have intimate fellowship with God, we know Him beyond mere surface-level knowledge. There are different types of relationships, and not all of them are intimate. Some are merely casual or based on mutual convenience. The Father longs for a close relationship with us. He does not want a superficial acquaintance; He wants intimacy. Intimacy with God leads us to the Most Holy Place—the deepest, most sacred place in God, where we are transformed, sanctified, and receive all that He desires to give us. We must pay a price to obtain this kind of intimacy. Not everyone is willing to pay it.

PRAYER IS THE MEANS OF DEVELOPING AN INTIMATE RELATIONSHIP WITH GOD.

Many people want something from God, but they do not want to make the effort to develop a meaningful relationship with Him. It is impossible to be in real communication with the Lord if we haven't established such fellowship. If our prayer life is not founded on intimacy, then our relationship with God, on our part, is merely based on expediency. This does not please God. The level of intimacy between us and the Father is a good gauge of the state of our heart and how prepared we are for Jesus's coming. Those who maintain a great hunger for more of God are a rare, supernatural people. The Lord will only return for a remnant that has a deep relationship with Him and a lifestyle of worship.

PRAYER IS TWO-WAY COMMUNICATION WITH GOD.

SEEK THE SPIRIT'S INFILLING DAILY

Another indispensable part of the remnant's preparation is to seek the infilling of the Holy Spirit daily so that we can stay continuously filled. Some people ask, "If I have already been baptized and filled with the Spirit, what need is there for more?" There is no such thing as an infilling that lasts forever. A one-time filling is not enough to keep our lamps burning. Our filling must be regularly replenished. This is the pattern we see in the book of Acts. The apostles and other believers in the early church were continuously filled with the Holy Spirit. (See, for example, Acts 2:4; 4:8, 31; 9:17; 13:9, 52.)

Moreover, Paul exhorted, "*Do not grieve the Holy Spirit of God, by whom you were sealed for the day of redemption*" (Ephesians 4:30), "*Do not be drunk with wine, in which is dissipation; but be filled with the Spirit*" (Ephesians 5:18), and "*Do not quench the Spirit*" (1 Thessalonians 5:19). If we stray from God, ignoring His Word, we may grieve His Spirit. Any time this occurs, we must immediately repent and receive a fresh infilling.

When we cease to be filled with the Spirit, our old fallen nature, rather than our redeemed spirit, begins to take control of our life. We lose the power to continuously die to our old nature. (See, for example, Ephesians 4:22.) Those of us who are leaders in ministry frequently need to be refilled because we are always giving to and serving others. The oil of the Spirit that we carry is constantly being poured out, requiring fresh anointings.

Again, the five foolish virgins were left out of the wedding feast when the bridegroom arrived because they had not kept their lamps filled with oil, which represents the infilling and power of the Holy Spirit. The Spirit is the oil that lights our lamps! Thus, the remnant bride can only maintain its connection with the Bridegroom by being filled with the Holy Spirit.

Jesus compared our need for the Holy Spirit to our natural thirst for water:

> *Now on the last and most important day of the feast, Jesus stood and called out [in a loud voice], If anyone is thirsty, let him come to Me and drink! He who believes in Me [who adheres to, trusts in, and relies on Me], as the Scripture has said, 'From his innermost being will flow continually rivers of living water.'" But He was speaking of the [Holy] Spirit, whom those who believed in Him [as Savior] were to receive afterward. The Spirit had not yet been given, because Jesus was not yet glorified (raised to honor).* (John 7:37–39 AMP)

THERE IS ONLY ONE BAPTISM IN THE HOLY SPIRIT, BUT THERE ARE MANY FILLINGS OF THE SPIRIT.

Living things need water in order to function properly and stay alive. The Holy Spirit is the supernatural water from which we must daily drink and be filled. *"Deep calls unto deep at the noise of Your water-falls; all Your waves and billows have gone over me"* (Psalm 42:7). Without this fullness, we cannot function spiritually. Our spirits become dry and our senses become dull until, eventually, spiritual death occurs. This is why it is essential for us to be continually filled with the Holy Spirit if we are to be prepared for the coming of the Lord.

WILL YOU RESPOND TO THE CALL?

The Holy Spirit is calling us—you, me, and all believers—to prepare for the coming of the Lord Jesus. Who will listen to Him? Who will answer His call? Will you respond by seeking holiness? Will you vigilantly watch and pray? Will you witness and serve with a sense of urgency? Will you cultivate an intimate relationship with God? Will you daily seek to be filled with the Holy Spirit?

The call is being made today—here and now. No one else can respond for you. Only you can answer the cry of the Holy Spirit to the members of the remnant bride who will lay down their lives to prepare the way for Christ's coming. If you will respond to this call, pray the following prayer:

Heavenly Father, I come into Your presence with a heavy heart. I recognize that I have not been watching, praying, or proclaiming the gospel with a sense of urgency. My relationship with You has grown cold. It is not as intimate as it used to be. It has been a long time since I have had a fresh filling of Your Holy Spirit. I want to respond to the call of the Spirit and be part of the glorious bride whom Christ seeks. I want Jesus to take me with Him in the rapture! I don't want to remain on earth and go through the tribulation.

Holy Spirit, I ask You to fill me with Your presence. Ignite me with Your holy fire! Purify me! Sanctify me! I pledge to turn from worldly thinking and behavior and to consecrate myself to the Lord, seeking His presence day and night and serving Him with my time, family, gifts, money, and everything else that I have received from His hand. Holy Spirit, empower me with Your anointing, Your grace, Your holiness, Your vision, Your revelation, and Your wisdom. I declare that I am part of God's holy remnant. In Jesus's name, amen!

Jesus is coming soon. Prepare the way of the Lord!

SUMMARY

+ The Holy Spirit is calling all members of God's remnant to dedicate themselves to Christ so they may prepare the way for His coming.

+ Jesus paid the price of our ransom from sin, fully redeeming us. Now, He refines us so that He can present us to Himself as a pure bride.

+ The remnant is glorious, without spot or wrinkle; it is holy, undefiled, separate from the world, and dedicated exclusively to be the bride of Christ.

+ Christ desires a glorious, holy, and pure bride not because of some arbitrary reason but because these qualities are foundational to His own nature.

+ The bride is consecrated to God and has sanctified herself to hear His voice, obey Him, and serve Him. She walks according to the Spirit's counsel and advances with His power to spread the kingdom of God on earth.

+ Indispensable steps for preparing for Christ's return include the following: allow Jesus to purify and consecrate you, keep vigilant, maintain a sense of urgency, cultivate an intimate relationship with God, and seek the Spirit's infilling daily.

SIGNS OF THE TIMES TESTIMONIES

SUPERNATURAL VISION AND PROVISION

Jesus and Nathalie Guerrero live in Miami, Florida, United States, and are members of King Jesus Ministry. They went through a difficult process in which God formed their character and led them to spiritual maturity. Today, they are not only business leaders but also leaders in the church. They are involved in End Time Investors, a program at King Jesus Ministry that raises funds to take the kingdom message to more and more areas of the world. They recognize the urgency of reaching the lost in these last days and are investing their own time to do their part. Nathalie gives their testimony:

I am a product of the vision of King Jesus Ministry. I came to this church when I was twelve years old, but I lived a worldly lifestyle until I was nineteen. One day, a woman in the church prophesied over me, and I decided to give my heart to Christ. Jesus set me free and changed me, giving me a purpose for my life. In time, my husband and I, who were married at the church, became mentors and leaders of a House of Peace. We were also blessed to start our own business, and today we own several businesses. When we began, we had one employee, but now we have almost thirty. We expanded because we believed God would honor every pledge we made to Him and every prophetic word of multiplication we had received.

Recently, the Lord spoke to my husband about making a pledge to provide money to help construct the House of Prayer for All Nations, which King Jesus Ministry is building. God said, "If you will give toward My house, I will pay for yours." We planted a $100,000 seed, giving it with complete conviction. Within four months, the $2.4 million house we were constructing was paid off without any loans from the bank. Not only that, but, at the time, we were living in a house worth $610,000, and the Lord enabled us to pay for it in full after we made another financial commitment toward His work. We have no debt!

When I first came to King Jesus Ministry, I had some erroneous mindsets and attitudes that needed to be renewed. My thoughts about my potential were limited. I barely dreamed of living in a small apartment and being a teacher. But God has given me vision and direction to pursue endeavors I never imagined possible because He has a plan for me during these end times.

A couple of years ago, I experienced another supernatural intervention. I was struggling with the idea of going to law school, and during an event at the church, the Lord confirmed this plan by saying, "Go study law." I finally decided to obey Him. Even though I didn't study hard enough for the preliminary exam, I passed it, and I ended up at the top of my class.

My peaceful home life is another product of God's love. My children fear God and are excellent at what they do. In addition, my marriage has changed so much! My husband and I used to be verbally abusive and disrespectful toward one another, and our relationship was worldly. Even though we were involved in ministry, we reached a point where we wanted to get divorced. However, we went through a very difficult process in which the Lord restored our marriage.

Our healthy family life, prosperous businesses, and involvement as End Time Investors are due to God's mercy and our obedience in applying various kingdom principles, which have led to many blessings. We are watching and praying for the coming of the Lord, but we are also busy doing His work so that when He comes, He will find us bearing much fruit.

HEALED OF A DISEASE THAT HAS NO CURE

Pastor Paola Ramos of Richmond, Virginia, United States, was diagnosed with trigeminal neuralgia. This disease has no known medical cure. However, during these end times, the Lord has increased His power on the earth to heal the impossible.

I came to this country when I was expecting my first child. At the beginning of the pregnancy, I began to feel discomfort in my face, but my doctors could not diagnose the problem. Meanwhile, the pain intensified. I tried various painkillers, none of which worked. Toward the end of the pregnancy, I was losing weight, which affected the baby. I couldn't eat or sleep, and I was worried that I was hurting my daughter's life!

After I gave birth, I went through a series of tests. It took a full year before I received a diagnosis of trigeminal neuralgia, a chronic condition in which pain radiates from the face to the brain. I felt pain from my ears to my eyes and along my entire jawline. I even felt pain in my teeth. My facial nerves were always swollen. I started taking an antiepileptic drug and became so dependent on this drug that it became my god. I needed medication just to be able to eat!

Trigeminal neuralgia causes indescribable pain! Some people have killed themselves to stop the agony. For me, there came a time when the medicine was no longer enough to dull the pain. I used to take four pills a day just to function. However, I couldn't keep up the necessary dosage, and the pain wouldn't let up; it was increasing daily. Although I didn't want to lose hope, I was at the breaking point. The doctors wanted to operate on me.

Even before my diagnosis, I had asked God to heal me, but nothing happened. I had been a Christian for many years and my faith had grown. I had seen God do many miracles, but I was still sick. I began to doubt and question the Lord, asking Him, "Why don't You want to heal me?" I didn't know what to think. I was disappointed and couldn't understand why I had to go through this ordeal. Life had become so difficult that I didn't want to do anything anymore, including my duties as a mother and wife. Although I was a pastor, I could no longer serve God or His people. I couldn't even open my mouth to sing or worship without feeling pain. My life was stagnant!

Even so, at that time, my heart's desire was to have another child. The doctors told me that as long as I was on medication, I should not become pregnant because the baby might develop genetic problems. I decided to take a step of faith and believe God. I went to King Jesus Ministry and asked the prophet Ana Maldonado for prayer. When she prayed for me, I said to God in my heart, "Lord, Your will be done." Right there, I knew God had done something. I didn't see any change in my condition until two months later when I felt something kick in my womb. I was pregnant! At first, I was scared, but the doctors examined me and said my baby was in perfect condition. To God be the glory! Today, I no longer need to take medication, and I don't feel any pain. God has healed me. It amazes me how, even during my trials and doubts, God was faithful to restore my faith and His promises in my life.

ABOUT
THE AUTHOR

Apostle Guillermo Maldonado is the senior pastor and founder of King Jesus International Ministry (Ministerio Internacional El Rey Jesus) in Miami, Florida, a multicultural church considered to be one of the fastest growing in the United States. King Jesus Ministry, whose foundation is built upon the Word of God, prayer, and worship, currently has a membership of more than 25,000 in the United States, including the main church in Miami, its campuses, its daughter churches, and its online church. Apostle Maldonado is also a spiritual father to 500 churches in 70 countries throughout the United States, Latin America, Europe, Africa, Asia, and New Zealand, which form the Supernatural Global Network, representing more than 750,000 people. In addition, he is the founder of the University of the Supernatural Ministry (USM). The building of kingdom leaders and the visible manifestations of God's supernatural power distinguish the ministry as the number of its members constantly multiplies.

A national best-selling author, Apostle Maldonado has written over fifty books and manuals, many of which have been translated into other languages. His books with Whitaker House include *Jesus Is Coming Soon, Created for Purpose, Breakthrough Prayer, Breakthrough Fast, Stress-Free Living, How to Walk in the Supernatural Power of God, The Glory of God, The Kingdom of Power, Supernatural Transformation, Supernatural Deliverance,* and *Divine Encounter with the Holy Spirit,* all of which are available in both English and Spanish. In addition, he preaches the message of Jesus Christ and His redemptive power on his international television program, *The Supernatural Now* (*Lo sobrenatural ahora*), which airs on TBN, Daystar, the Church Channel, and fifty other networks, with a potential outreach and impact to more than two billion people around the world.

Apostle Maldonado has a doctorate in Christian counseling from Vision International University and a master's degree in practical theology from Oral Roberts University. He resides in Miami, Florida, with his wife and ministry partner, Ana, and their two sons, Bryan and Ronald.

Welcome to Our House!

We Have a Special Gift for You

It is our privilege and pleasure to share in your love of Christian books. We are committed to bringing you authors and books that feed, challenge, and enrich your faith.

To show our appreciation, we invite you to sign up to receive a specially selected **Reader Appreciation Gift**, with our compliments. Just go to the Web address at the bottom of this page.

God bless you as you seek a deeper walk with Him!

WE HAVE A GIFT FOR YOU. VISIT:

whpub.me/nonfictionthx

WHITAKER
HOUSE